Inside

MW00416219

Reflections of a Parish Priest

By Reverend Francis J. Peffley

To Janet,
God Bless you
And your Family!
Fr. Fran Peffley

God's Perfect Dream

If every man were Joseph,

And every woman Mary,

And every child were Jesus brought to birth,

O how their peace would heal the hurts of
earth,

And humankind rejoice to find its worth!

Were every father Joseph,

And every mother Mary,

And each new life a Christ-Child from the
start,

How soon the curse of evil would depart

And goodness grow again in every heart!

O let each man be Joseph,

And every woman Mary,

And every child be Jesus come anew:

That love may live in everything we do

And God's great dream of Galilee comes
true!

Nihil Obstat: Rev. Thomas J. Lehning, Ph.D.

Censor Librorum

Imprimatur: + Paul S. Loverde

Bishop of Arlington

March 10, 2015

Acknowledgments

Dedicated in loving memory to my parents
Bill and Mary Peffley, whose 58 years of
marriage has been an inspiration to myself
and to my sisters Edel and Natia.

Poems by

Bill Peffley

Used with permission

Scripture quotations from

The New American Bible, Revised Edition

(NABRE)

Copyright 2010

I. Sailing the Seven Cs of Matrimony

Looking Back

The burnished chest of long ago,

in which we stored our hearts,

has silvered in the twilight glow;

(Though sheen of youth departs,

it shimmers on in memory . . .)

The garment-years we've worn

became a sacred tapestry,

wear-patched but never torn.

What of the hearts within the box?

What has enclosure done?

Made diamonds of life's stumbling blocks,

pressed two hearts into one.

Sailing the Seven Cs of Matrimony

There was a newly ordained priest who was very nervous about doing his very first wedding, so he asked the elderly monsignor for help. "Monsignor, what do I do if I go blank?   Or if I lose my place?" The monsignor sagely replied, "Just quote a scripture passage. Have a gospel quote ready to use and that will help you find your place again." The wedding day arrived and the new priest was officiating at his first wedding. All went well up to the homily when he went completely blank and frantically realized he had never prepared a scripture quote! His planned homily just wasn't there! Not a single word would come! He breathed a pleading prayer to the Holy Spirit for a scripture verse. Staring out at the large congregation and turning his gaze toward the waiting couple, he said the first words of scripture that came to mind: "Father, forgive them; they know not what they do!"(Lk 23:34).

There is one place with regard to

marriage where this particular scripture quote might be applied. Did you know the average engaged couple spends 200 hours preparing for the wedding ceremony and only eight hours in preparation for a lifetime of marriage? This does not promise "smooth sailing" for any engaged couple. This condition needs to be reversed. We need to have couples spending appropriate time preparing for a lifetime marriage. So let me take you on a "cruise"; on what I call the "Seven Cs of Matrimony," seven qualities that help ensure a happy marriage.

I base these following observations on several things: my own parents' fifty-eight years of marriage; my twenty-seven years of Catholic priesthood; the pleasure I've had of getting to know thousands of wonderful Catholic couples, whose thoughts on marriage I'm going to share with you, and the privilege of instructing over 800 couples preparing for the Sacrament as well as the opportunity to do about 40 weddings a year for the last twenty years of my priesthood!

The first of the Seven Cs is a Calling,

a vocation. Marriage is a vocation, a calling from God. The word vocation comes from the Latin, *vocare*, which means to call. Priests and nuns are not the only ones who have a vocation from God; everybody has a unique vocation from Almighty God. There is the priesthood, religious life and single life in the world, but the majority of people God calls to enter into the Holy Sacrament of Marriage.

With regard to this topic of vocation and its various expressions, there is the overall, universal vocation to holiness, which everyone is called to - the vocation to become a saint, to get to heaven. It's the one vocation everyone has! God made his human creatures to know him, to love him and to serve him, in order for them to be happy forever in eternity. It's the ultimate vocation for everyone, regardless of their state in life. St. Therese, the Little Flower, said we should have one goal in life - to become a saint. When you think about it, it makes common sense to aim high for heaven, because if you do come up a little short, there's always the safety of purgatory! And Bishop Sheen says, "Don't aim just for purgatory, because if you come up short there, you know where you're going to land!"

But now for the vocation of the Holy Sacrament of Matrimony. The foundation upon which to build a marriage is prayer, serious prayer, that God will send the right person to marry. It certainly will make life a lot easier for the next thirty, forty or fifty years if you marry the right person! This means sincere prayer for a future spouse, for the one God has intended you to marry. You don't want to be like the person Zig Ziglar, motivational speaker and author, met on one of his flights. Sitting next to him was a man whom he noticed had what resembled a wedding band on his index finger. During their eventual polite chatter, when the man answered "yes" to the question, "Is that a wedding band you're wearing?" Zig asked why he wore it on the wrong finger? "Because I married the wrong woman!" was the reply. Faithful prayer for a faithful future spouse is a necessity.

Prayer is also necessary in the dating process, prayerful discernment about the prospective one who has come along, and who may hold the promise of a blessed future in marriage. Special prayer is needed, in particular silent time in Eucharistic Adoration. Is this the person You want me to marry? Is this the person You have sent who will help get me to heaven? Is this the person that You want me to help to get to heaven, the spouse who will be open to life and who will be my partner leading our children to their calling to holiness? Discernment is talking things over with God and his Mother.

The most important thing in the universal call to holiness and to the vocation of marriage is being in a state of grace, in the state of friendship with God. By being in a state of grace, living the life of grace, one is able to make the right decisions due to the indwelling presence of the Blessed Trinity - Father, Son and Holy Spirit - within the soul; This means entitlement to the gifts and virtues and graces of the Holy Spirit, to be able to know who it is that God wants to be

12

together in marriage. To prepare for every vocation it is necessary to spend time in silence, in Eucharistic Adoration, and in personal contact with God in prayer.

The second C ingredient of a happy marriage is Compatibility. It is obvious that couples are attracted to one another, and it's usually compatible couples that end up in marriage. This compatibility should first and foremost be found in their common faith in Jesus Christ, and if possible, their faith in the Church, being members of the Catholic Church.

But of course there are other aspects of compatibility that are involved. Dating time, sharing common activities and interests such as music, sports or restaurants, add to the development of compatibility. But the difference in personality should be noted. Realize that there are four different types of people: the popular, the powerful, the perfectionist and the peaceful. Typically a person doesn't usually marry someone who has the same temperament. Oftentimes, a strong-willed person will marry an easygoing

13

one, and the more outgoing person a more introverted one. It is my recommendation that when dealing with the topic of compatibility, that some reading and study of the four temperaments be done. It is my experience that marriages are specially blessed and more deeply peaceful when the couples understand the importance of knowing each other's temperament. I recommend the books by Art and Laraine Bennett - The Temperament God Gave You, The Temperament God Gave Your Spouse - as ideal sources for reading and studying the four temperaments.

Although there are seven Cs to the main theme of this chapter, I have more Cs to add under the quality of compatibility. When helping to prepare couples for marriage I like to emphasize these important points that will aid them in their work of compatibility.

1) Practice showing courtesy, consideration and kindness to each other, treat each other as the most important person on the face of the earth! This makes for a happy marriage. It is said that if we treated people at work the way we treat people at

home, we would probably not have too many friends! (And possibly be out of a job, as well!)

The sentiment in the old song, Little Things Mean a Lot, seems to have been written for marriage: it seldom prospers without attention to the little things. There are many examples: using words like "thank you" or "God bless you"; taking out the trash without being asked, cooking his favorite dish unexpectedly, holding the car door for her, or not asking him to help with the dishes!

Remembering birthdays and anniversaries in a special way is a good place to start. I remember a sign in a florists shop over the refrigerated roses; it had sets of three roses, six roses, and twelve roses and the sign simply said, "Just how mad did you make her?" Three? Six? Twelve? So giving the wife a dozen roses now and then is a great idea. A box of chocolates never hurts either! (Just ignore the comment about the weight!)

2) More Cs! When preparing couples for marriage I am amazed at how many are going into marriage with a credit card debt of

ten to fifteen thousand dollars at huge interest rates! Getting to understand the area of finance: currency, cash and credit cards is a must! In surveys of divorced couples ages twenty to thirty, 85% said the number one cause for their break-up was problems over money. Some study of finance and good stewardship is a fundamental requirement for a happy marriage, and it begins with a careful use of the credit card. One husband said, "I had to do plastic surgery on my wife - I took away her credit card for a few weeks!" A wife described how they froze their credit card in a block of ice, to slow them down when they wanted to buy something; they often found that by the time the ice melted they actually didn't need what they were thinking of buying! Very simply, my brilliant wisdom on the subject of keeping out of debt is to spend less than you make! It took me all night to come up with that! And then there is the observation that many people have too much month left at the end of their money.

Jim Rohn, another motivational author, suggests his philosophy of "70-20-

10": Try to live on 70% of your income, save or invest 20% and give 10% to charity. And he recommends giving 10% to charity first. He gives the example of a young child's dollar allowance in the form of ten dimes. He explains that the first dime goes to the church or to the poor; the next two are dropped in the piggy bank and the remaining seven are all for spending.

This leads naturally to the subject of Tithing, the giving to God 10% of our wealth, that first 10%. This is a Biblical principle. In the Old Testament, when a king's subjects tithed to him, it was understood that the king had the responsibility for protecting their villages. Tithing today is a matter of trust, of relying on God to take special care of us, to take control of our finances. An accepted idea suggests the setting aside of one or two hundred dollars a month before facing the paying of the bills: pay God first, invest second, and live on the third part. Jim Rohn once said, "When your outgo exceeds your income, your upkeep becomes your downfall!" There are many great books available to help make sure finances do not become a problem in marriage.

3) Compatibility requires cooperation, working together as a team. We know from the sports world that T-E-A-M means Together Everyone Achieves More. Zig Ziglar gives the example of the Belgian horse which can, by itself, pull 8,000 pounds, but when two Belgian horses pull together the weight can be up to 18,000 pounds. And when they are trained to pull together the weight is 25, 000 pounds! This is a wonderful image for success in marriage. Working together as a team, always moving together in the same direction, increases the potential for harmony and happiness in marriage.

4) Then there is compromise. Not to be considered here is the compromising of Faith, Values or Virtue, but the compromising of self-will. Flexibility. Yielding self will always open the door to peace and restore reality to tense situations. A willow in a storm will bend; a telephone pole may crack and tear dangerous wires. What buildings survive earthquakes? The

ones with the built-in sway mechanism. Sometimes in a marriage there can be a 5.0 on the Richter scale or even an 8.2! Being flexible, being willing to compromise our own preferences, is the safety mechanism for marital peace, and when done from the motive of love of God is a springboard to mutual spiritual joy.

5) A final point under compatibility is courtship. Zig Ziglar has a whole book called Courtship after Marriage. The idea is to keep a link with the past, with some of the things that placed beauty and joy in the budding relationship. Keep a date together once a week or once a month   I love to tell my favorite story of a couple I've known for twenty-five years. They're still in love, they still hold hands.   When I asked the husband what he did to keep the romance alive in their marriage he said, "Father, I'll tell you. Each week for the last twenty-five years, my wife and I have gone to a little Italian restaurant which is incredibly romantic with a bottle of wine, music and dancing. By going there each week, it has kept our romance alive."

Then he added, "I go on Tuesdays, she goes on Fridays!" I said, "Are you kidding me?" He said, "Only about the last part - everything else is true." I encourage the couples at my parish to go out once a month on a date, to get a babysitter and spend time together, "like the good old days." It does wonders for both the couple and the marriage.

Moving on to the third ingredient necessary for a happy marriage I want to emphasize Communication, good communication, spending "quality" time with each other, being good listeners and giving each other sincere and genuine compliments. Remember Mark Twain's comment that he could survive two months on one good compliment? They say if you want to improve somebody's hearing, pay them a compliment. And it's amazing how poor people's hearing becomes when they're nagged! Take kids for example. Give them a compliment and you get their attention; boss them around and they tend to tune us out. Dale Carnegie had three words that he said people should avoid at all costs, which I apply to marriage: never complain, criticize, or condemn. (More Cs!) People say, 'What else is there to talk about?" Rather than complain, commend; rather than criticize, compliment; rather than condemn, condole.

Gary Smalley, an inspirational Protestant minister, has written several worthwhile books on marriage. I highly recommend for "Her" For Better or For Best, and for "Him" If Only He Knew. He says that the results of certain studies showed that the average man speaks 12,000 words a day, and the average woman 24,000 words a day. So you can imagine the scenario: The wife has had a quiet day at home alone with the new baby, where she used up only 200 of her 24,000 words, she still has 23,800 to go! The husband returning from work, having used up all his 12,000 words early in the day, is anticipating a quiet evening at home. You get the point!

One of Gary Smalley's most important points is that couples should be careful not to close each other's spirit by

21

inadvertently being insulting or offending in some way. Spouses don't want to be like the husband who says to his wife, "Honey, I can't believe how God could make someone so beautiful and yet so dense," and she retorts, "Well, I agree that God made me beautiful so you would fall in love with me and I believe God made me dense so I would fall in love with you!"

Sometimes, in a group of people, the husband may jokingly say something like this: "My wife treats me like a God, every morning she places burnt offerings before me!" He might get a laugh, but how does it affect his wife's heart? Chi Chi Rodriguez, the great golfer, said, "I attribute becoming a millionaire to marrying my wife. Before I met her, I was a multimillionaire!" Again, those things can be funny, but they can sometimes close a person's heart or wound a person's spirit. Realizing the power of words and the need to be careful not to hurt each other's feelings is the cornerstone of marital communication. Take Zig Ziglar's reminder: "If you gripe about the mashed potatoes at dinner, all you can expect for the rest of the evening is a cold shoulder!"

Commitment is the fourth and bedrock of these "Seven Cs of Matrimony" - total commitment until death. Partial commitment cannot be considered. In our society today getting married is very challenging, with fifty percent of ordinary couples getting divorced. That's why we need extraordinary couples! Only extraordinary couples will survive, only good families, heroic families can win out against these odds. One of the signs of our cultural decay is the frequency of pre-nuptial agreements; the marriage is pre-conditioned by agreement of both parties to the division of rights and property should a divorce occur. Couples who go into marriage with prenuptial agreements usually end up in divorce court. I was told that within ten years of marriage with a prenuptial agreement, 95% end in divorce. Marriage is not a contract or a "deal"; it is a donation of self to the other until death. To allow for the possibility of divorce in the beginning is often the beginning of the end! Divorce is not a word in the dictionary of married love.

In fact, it is recommended that it never be mentioned. The priest who married my parents, when he heard my Dad kiddingly say, "She's a good cook, Father, I think I'll keep her!" gave them a stern warning to never refer to divorce in any way in their married life, for it would admit of its possibility! (A few years ago I said the 60th Anniversary Mass for a couple in their early eighties. It was a beautiful event. I asked the husband his opinion of divorce and marriage. He said, "Father, in these sixty years of marriage I never once contemplated divorce; murder often, but never divorce!")

With commitment comes the need for perseverance. Perseverance has been defined as Commitment in Action. That means a daily willing to succeed. In marriage, love is in the will. The man who has left his wife and claims he "doesn't love her any more" is admitting he doesn't want to love her any more. At the end of his life, Winston Churchill was asked the secret of his success.

He replied with seven words, "Never give up. Never, never give up." And that can be an ideal motto for marriage. Someone has said, "Always give in (to each other) but never give up (the dream)."

There are many examples of the spirit of perseverance that can be inspiring for married couples: Walt Disney went broke seven times during his life; they were building blocks of his success. There's the story of the Comstock Gold Mine, which the owners had been digging with no success for many years and sold for $7,000. The next owner dug five more feet and struck one of the largest gold mines in history. Thomas Edison used over 10,000 different filaments before he found the perfect one for the electric light bulb. When he was accused of failing 10,000 times he remarked, "Not true; I have successfully found 10,000 ways that would not work."

These examples of perseverance for material gain should alert married couples to the value of their supreme work of building and perfecting a holy, "successful" marriage and family.

The fifth of the seven Cs is an understanding of the mystery of The Cross. Every vocation has its crosses, toils and disappointments. I suppose you've heard of the Three Rings of Marriage? First comes the engagement ring, then the wedding ring, then the "suffer-ring." Suffering is a necessary element of the Christian life and is found in everyone's vocation - priests, nuns, and singles in the world. Usually, these must bear their crosses alone. The married have a helpmate. "If you wish to be a follower of mine, you must renounce yourself, take up your cross every day and follow in my footsteps" (Lk 9:23). Notice the wisdom of the Church. The marriage vows include the words "for better or worse, richer or for poorer, in sickness or in health until death do you part." I'm reminded of a parishioner who once said to me, "Father I didn't know you could be married sixteen times as a Catholic." I said, "What do you mean, sixteen times?" He quipped, "Four better, four worse, four richer, four poorer!"

26

This understanding of the mystery of the cross is the key to true happiness in every state of life. When suffering is accepted as an organic ingredient of married life the foundation is laid for permanent marital happiness and holiness. The suffering that comes to couples who try to avoid suffering is perhaps the saddest suffering of all, for they are living against the very grace needed to endure the trials and to succeed in marriage.

The Cross can take different forms and present many sacrifices in family life such as living on one income so the mother can be there for the children; living on a tighter budget, or in a smaller house than hoped for. Other sacrifices come to mind: severe financial difficulties, a sick parent or relative, a disabled child, or the difficulty of infertility (which one out of six couples experiences). There are millions of couples in America bearing the cross of waiting to hear from the adoption agency.

Or the cross might be just the opposite. To be very fertile and have to face

27

the challenge of following God's teachings on marriage and family in the encyclical Humanae Vitae, (the prophetic document of Pope Paul VI, which I encourage everyone to read) and to realize that artificial contraception is a serious sin, is one of the heaviest crosses couples could know. But it should be stated that of the couples that practice contraception, 50% end up getting divorced, whereas couples that follow God's teaching on marriage, that understand natural family planning and follow marriage God's way, less than 2% get divorced. Bishop Sheen said every time you see a child, you see the incarnation of the love between husband and wife, and know that that child did not exist at one point. God created that child with the husband and wife.

It is good to remember that the crosses we must carry have two sides. We see and feel only the suffering side, with all the physical, emotional, financial, relational or even spiritual pain and trials that come with them. With faith and trust in God, we can see behind the Cross, see the other side,

28

the side that faces eternity, where Grace and comfort and even joy are simultaneously present. Realize that with the cross comes grace, the grace to endure and to mature in love. Saint Louis de Montfort says that "the cross is filled with diamonds." (That is one reason it is heavy!) It is something of great value, something to cherish. Usually our crosses are blessings in disguise and oftentimes when we compare our crosses with those of other people, we realize how well off we are in carrying our own.

There is the story of the man who complained about the awkwardness and heaviness of his cross and asked the Lord for a different one. He was shown into a room stocked with thousands of crosses in every size, weight and length. The man searched, picked the smallest one he could find and took it to the Lord who smiled and said, "Good choice! That's the very cross you have been complaining about!"

So it's good to remember that every cross is custom-made for us, handpicked by Providence to fit our spiritual destiny. The cross of Good Friday had Easter Sunday on its other side!

The sixth C of a happy marriage is Charity. Charity means love, not just natural love, but supernatural love, charity that comes from God's grace. Jesus said, "Love one another as I have loved you" (Jn 13:34). Look at a crucifix - I mean really look at a crucifix - to see God's love for you. How did Jesus love? Totally, unconditionally, unselfishly, as Catholic married couples are called to do. Being God, he did not have to attach himself horribly to the cross, but he did so anyway, out of love. Married couples are also asked to do things they would rather not do; let the crucifix be the template of their love and let it be meditated upon often. Christ died on the cross for the sake of his beloved, the Church. And the Bible says, "Husbands love your wives, even as Christ loved the Church" (Eph 5:25). He loved the Church totally, unconditionally and unselfishly. If you want to see what the true symbol of love is, don't look at the arrowed heart on a Valentine, but at the crucifix - The symbol of Christ's total, sacrificial, self-donating love. No Catholic home should be without a crucifix as a permanent reminder of what true love is.

C.S. Lewis, in his book, The Four Loves, shows the levels of love available to the human heart. The first is "eros", which is romantic love; there is the Greek word "storge", which is affection; "philia", which is brotherly love, and finally "agape," which is sacrificial, unconditional love. It is agape that God wants us to have for one another, and especially for couples to have for each other.

Realize that love is much more than an emotion, much more than a feeling. Love is an act of the will. Love is a decision. I'm sure Jesus didn't feel like dying on the cross, but he did it as an act of love. Love is self-giving. One definition of love is to desire the highest good for the sake of the beloved, putting the other person first. As you know, Mother Teresa said joy is spelled J-O-Y: J for Jesus, O for Others and Y for yourself. Emotions and feelings come and go, but true love is a steady act of the will. That's why God can command us to love him with our whole heart, soul, strength and mind, and to love our neighbour as our self.

Where do we get the grace to love supernaturally? It must, of course, come from a supernatural source - it must come from Christ, truly present in the Blessed Sacrament of the Eucharist. If marriage is to be lived the way God intends, the Holy Eucharist is where to find that grace, in Mass and Holy Communion not only every Sunday but even every day if family obligations allow it. "I am the vine, you are the branches . . . without me, you can do nothing" (Jn 15:5). If spouses were to separate themselves from Christ by mortal sin, there is withering and death of the spiritual life, and a cutting of the graces necessary for their Calling; but, united to Christ, they can produce the grace to love each other in a supernatural, Christ-like, agape way. I recommend the pamphlet written by the Couple to Couple League called, Marriage and the Eucharist, on the five similarities

32

between the Eucharist and matrimony. Just as in the Eucharist we become one with Christ, so in marriage husbands and wives become one with each other.

The topic of Charity also includes forgiveness. The Bible cautions against letting "the sun go down on your anger" (Ep 4:26). Whatever the mistakes or misunderstandings of the day, the marriage covenant forbids prolonging a disagreement. Couples must be like Cortez and the conquistadors of old: once on the shore of the new world, they burned their boats, so committed they were to the new life. As Ken Blanchard says, "Don't gunny sack," don't carry a sack of old hurts. Petty disputes and hurt feelings are the boats that carry a dangerous cargo of division and alienation. They must be sunk at sunset. An Our Father said together with hands joined at the words "forgive us our trespasses as we forgive those who trespass against us" will be a direct hit at the pesky little boats the devil tries to sail into the tranquil waters of marriage.

And the last C - and by all means not

least! - is Christ. Bishop Sheen said it takes three to get married: the husband, the wife and Christ. In his book, Three to Get Married, Bishop Sheen says marriage is like a triangle, with Christ at the top and the husband and wife at the other two angles. The closer each spouse grows to Jesus, the closer they come to each other. The opposite is also true: if they drift away from Our Lord, they wind up farther apart. I've seen this happen in many marriages; one or the other gradually turns from God and eventually, they tend to turn away from each other.

As marriage can be seen as drawing a triangle toward Christ, it can also be considered a pyramid, resting upon the rock of Jesus Christ, and built by loving spouses into a Three-sided, long-lasting edifice of faithful marriage.

Security for a Catholic marriage depends upon the couple growing closer to Christ. This is done by fidelity to personal prayer, a daily life of prayer, and the sacramental life of Sunday or even daily

34

Mass and Communion, and confession at least once a month. Monthly confession can save marriages. In fact, it is my opinion that if husband and wife were to go to confession every month, they could solve any issue, any problem, because they will have the grace to love each other in a Christ-like way. Because of being joined in the Holy Sacrament of Marriage, they are living something sacred, something holy.

I wonder if married couples realize when they enter into marriage and make their wedding vows, that it may be the only Sacrament that they will actually administer? As a priest, I baptize babies, hear confessions and say Mass, but when I'm presiding at a wedding it's the couple who administers the Sacrament; I am just the witness. The two administer the Sacrament of Marriage to each other. This means they receive all the graces necessary for a holy, happy, enduring marriage. All the graces are there for an entire lifetime together. I call it the blank check of grace. One of the great weaknesses in otherwise good Christian marriages is that

35

the partners do not rely on the grace of the Sacrament. In other words, they don't trust Christ. Faith is lacking. If couples only realized the Presence of Christ is in each of them and in their marriage, that his Presence is a reality, an actuality, then all we have said about the Seven Cs would come to rest in this one final harbor. The acceptance of sacrifices, trials, and crosses would become intimate opportunities for growing in holiness. It is a faith to be longed for and prayed for every day and hour of married life. A wise priest once told a newly married couple: "Let the expression of your love for each other be the expression of your love for God." It's that real, and it's that easy. All the grace is there for an entire lifetime together.

II. A Priest's Look at Parenting

A Family Prayer

O God make us a family
To grow in You together,
To find You in each other
As the years go by;

Dear Lord, make us Your family
To share Your Life together,
To give You to each other
As the seasons fly.

Let us become true family
That we may be
Your Love run free
Along the chosen way You will we go;

O make us, Lord, a family,
To live in You forever,
To give to You together
All we come to be:

Your Life,
Your Love,
Your Family.

A Priest's Look at Parenting

A father, coming home after a hard day's work and hoping to relax and enjoy some peace and quiet, headed for his favorite chair and evening paper, only to meet his seven year old son running to him with the usual barrage of questions. The father, seeking to clear this obstacle to the pleasure of his chair and paper, had an idea. He opened the newspaper to the weather map of the United States, pulled it out, and carefully tore the map into a couple dozen pieces. "This is a game", he said, as he handed the pieces to his son; "See if you can tape this map of the United States together." The boy ran off excited about his new project, while the father sat back to enjoy his peace and quiet. To his surprise the boy was back in no time with the perfectly taped-together map. The father was amazed and asked how he had done it so quickly. "I was having trouble at first," said the boy, "but then I noticed that on the back of the map was a picture of a family.

38

So I put the family back together and the United States took care of itself!" The father realized the significance of this insightful remark and gave his son a big hug! This scenario holds several lessons for parents of today. There exists the too common attitude of parents whose personal preferences often ignore or exclude the needs of their children, whether physical, emotional, or spiritual - an evasion of opportunity for bonding with the child - which does not match the touching symbol of the family as the basic unit of society: a well-built family means a well-built nation.

Parents have one of the most challenging and at the same time rewarding of all vocations, with a variety of challenges and goals, the dominant goal being the achievement of Excellence in Parenting. To maintain a continual desire to grow in knowledge and experience in this special vocation is a superb quest, and as an aid to this quest, let me suggest what I like to call the Twelve As of Parenting, qualities I have found in my personal experience in relating with couples in successful marriages and families.

Affection.

Parents should be genuinely affectionate with their children since this gives the children the "hands on" experience of being loved. There were studies at the beginning of the last century in which infants were fed from a bottle but were deprived of any human touch or affection. The babies began to die, so the experiment had to be stopped. Children need actual physical contact from caring others to keep up their life and health. Expressed love through tenderness and physical affection is needed, as with proper nutrition needed for the body, to help develop them mentally, psychologically and spiritually. Another interesting study found that, until age one, boys receive the same amount of affection as do little girls, but boys from year one get about one-sixth the amount of affection that is given to girls. It's also a fact that boys get into trouble about six times more frequently than do girls (though, sadly, I observe that in this present culture and society the girls are catching up!). Some psychologists are of the opinion that there is a connection between the amount of affection boys receive and the amount of trouble they get into. My experience as a priest interacting with parish families leads me to believe that children who receive lots of affection from their parents feel better about themselves and will not be as trouble-bent as frequently as children deprived of that affection. One psychologist says that a child needs four hugs a day for survival, eight hugs a day for mental health, and twelve hugs a day for solid emotional growth. I always suggest that each child be given the maximum dose! Furthermore, recent studies have shown that people who receive lots of affection are healthier, happier, and have a stronger immune system. (Think of the medical bills that can be avoided by parents who take the time to hold their children's hand, or put an arm around them, let alone giving those hugs!) Affection is, of course, also shown through kind words and smiles. Expressions

41

like: *Good job! I love you. I'm proud of you!* can do so much good for a child's self-esteem. Loving eye contact must accompany these expressions and the smiles. Unfortunately, most parents give their children eye contact only when scolding or reprimanding. Looking lovingly into children's eyes and smiling at them fills their emotional tanks with reserves of self esteem and the ability for responsive love.

Teenagers, in their difficult and adjustment years, need a lot of affection and tenderness from their parents. Fathers especially need to be affectionate with their daughters during their teen years. Everyone craves affection, and if girls don't receive this primary male affection from their dads there may be a tendency to seek it from some other male. This is possibly one reason why some girls become promiscuous – they crave male affection, not primarily a physical act. There have been many studies in recent years seeking the underlying causes for homosexuality in both men and women; in this regard, Zig Ziglar, popular writer on friendship and family, states that the chances of homosexual development are reduced in teenage sons whose fathers are affectionate with them, indicating that aloof, unaffectionate fathers and dominant mothers contribute to homosexual tendencies in boys. I have met fathers who shy away from hugging their son, thinking they will "make a sissy out of him", but the research shows just the opposite

Acceptance.

Children need to be shown unconditional love, accepted for who they are: a blessing and a gift from God. Each son or daughter is also a son or daughter of God. When children are loved unconditionally it gives them a strong sense of security, an assurance that they are loved no matter what they do or what happens in their life. That's the kind of love God has for us, and sometimes we don't realize or fully appreciate the reality of that fact. God *is* love, and there is nothing that we can do to diminish his love for us. He might not like what we do, but he loves us still. Parents might not like what their children do, but they need to know - no matter what - that they are sincerely loved. By doing this they expose the children to an authentic and attractive image of God. Some Christian writers denote that it is crucial for the children that they get this true initial sense of what God is like from their parents. If they are loving, forgiving, kind and honest, their children will have an easier time thinking of God the Father that way. When parents are strict and uncaring, it seems to be that much harder for the children to visualize God in any other terms. So, particularly when children are young, mothers and fathers must realize that, together, they are a living and complete image of God to them. Setting limits and applying discipline is, of course, necessary, since it prepares the children for keeping the Ten Commandments and understanding authority, but this must be balanced by the awareness that parents are called to be, for their children, the mirror image of God, an image easily distorted when unconditional love, for all concerned, is missing from the home.

Approval.

All children need lots of honest compliments. Mark Twain wrote, "I can last a month on one good compliment." The poet says being generous with compliments to children is like watering the flowers of a garden. All children have good and bad qualities – flowers and weeds – growing in their garden of self. Parents have the continual job of watering their flowers and pulling up their weeds. Unfortunately, some parents seldom water and never weed the gardens of their children, and unwittingly reinforce negative traits instead of positive ones. "Why are you so messy?" or "Why aren't you as smart as your sister?" definitely water the weeds! Praising a child's good qualities generates healthy blossoming and increases the child's self-worth. There is a saying: "What gets praised gets repeated". If you see your children doing something praiseworthy –

being punctual, being kind to a brother or sister or friend, being generous – praise at that moment is sure to imbed those qualities in their character.

For praise and compliments to be most effective, I have found these few points to be beneficial. Praise must be sincere: insincere praise is easily detected - especially by kids - for what it is and is never appreciated. Praise should be specific: Children shouldn't just be told they're "great" - we should find a specific quality or action that is praiseworthy and mention it. Praise should be immediate: timing is everything; if a child is praised weeks after an achievement, it will have little impact. One rose on the day of an anniversary is better than a dozen later on! A great way to praise people is through others. Many bosses will compliment an employee by giving compliments to the employee's spouse, knowing they are sure to be delivered! I'm sure that most people have noticed, when talking directly to children, that they often give the impression of not listening. But let them hear you speaking of them from another room, or to a friend on the phone, and see how quickly their attention is caught! It is wise if God is brought into the praise, by using phrases like, "God has given my child a beautiful gift of being kind to others". In this way encouragement is given to the children and glory is given to God.

Attention.

A survey report from the American Parent-Teachers Association a few years ago estimated that the average American father spends less than two minutes a week in focused, one-on-one attention with his infant. The typical American father also spends less than seven minutes per week in focused attention with his teenager. Focused attention is defined as time spent without the TV or IPod being on at the same time. Many parents take courses to learn how to detect where their teenagers stand with drugs; more time spent with their kids and they soon would be able to tell! It is common knowledge that we pay attention to what we value and ignore what we don't. When real attention is paid to kids they subconsciously sense they are important and have value, and one of the best ways to show children they are valued is to really listen. Listening does three things: First, listening creates a bond of trust between the two who are communicating. It doesn't work if the child is speaking and we only half listen. Second, listening builds character in the listener; self-control is necessary to keep from interrupting! This is because the mind thinks at a rate of 400-500 words per minute while the voice can only produce about 150-200 words per minute. The listener is generally thinking two to three times faster than the speaker can talk. And third, listening intently to children without interruption is an unspoken compliment to them and is an occasion for the building of their self-esteem and sense of self-worth.

Appreciation.

Appreciation, of course, is shown by genuine gratitude, as expressed by thanking children for what they do - even the agreed upon chores like washing dishes, taking out the trash, or helping around the house. Being thanked makes a person feel important. In his book, *The One Minute Manager*, Ken Blanchard suggests that employers should "catch their employees doing something right" and immediately tell them they are doing a good job. This positive reinforcement may pleasantly surprise them. since employers are often perceived as policemen! It seems the common human practice to ignore people who are doing things right but to quickly notice those who do something wrong! Spencer Johnson, in his book, *The One Minute Father,* says that these same principles of successful management also apply to being a successful parent. "Catch your children doing something right" and thank them for it.

Admiration.

Admiration is acknowledging in others good qualities or traits; it is how virtue is fostered in children. Parents should be on the lookout for signs of faith, generosity, punctuality, kindness or any other good quality and "water" them by specific admiration. The next step up is to help them develop the theological virtues of faith, hope and charity and the cardinal virtues of prudence, justice, fortitude and temperance. Parents should acquaint themselves with these virtues by reading up on them from the catechism, so as to be aware of them in their child's behavior. These virtues would not usually be apparent in their classical form but can be assimilated into many occasions of family living. A child may show a certain quality of "common sense" in a situation, or indicate a desire to overcome a fear of facing some incident at school - which can be connected to the "big" virtues by an admiring or encouraging comment. This is one of the major aspects of the goal of Excellence in Parenting, preparing the child for heaven. With this admiration given to children we nourish their spiritual life and open them more and more to the plan God has for their sanctity in adult Christian life.

The Apology.

A mother or father whose goal is Excellence in Parenting is one who can apologize. In normal family life situations come up in which impatience or anger are inevitable; these experiences must always be rounded out with an apology, especially to the children. Telling the child "I'm sorry" is a powerful virtue in the parent and a lesson in love and holiness for the child. Apologizing teaches children courage, for it is often far from easy to admit a weakness and to say we're sorry. It also teaches children humility, and supplies them with the template for what to do when they do something wrong. This is a good preparation for the Sacrament of Reconciliation for young children, when they will tell God they are sorry for having offended him, and instills in older children a spiritual stamina for being good. If children see their parents apologizing for social or emotional weaknesses, it is much easier for them to

51

allow for their own fragile moments of human weakness and act accordingly.

Availability.

The above principles will work only if parents are willing to spend time with their children. T-I-M-E is the way kids spell LOVE. Family quality moments only come during periods of quantity time spent together. There's no need for parents to take their children to spectacular attractions like Disney World; small things like taking a walk, playing games, or taking an ice cream break can do a great deal toward fostering a healthy parent-child bond. Occasionally, when we were growing up, our dad would set aside a special day for me and my two sisters, a day for each of us individually. We would pick what we wanted to do – I'd pick fishing, or a train ride to see the historic and religious sights of Philadelphia, or a major league ballgame – and each sister would choose places like the Doll Museum, a movie after lunch at a special restaurant, or a shopping trip – whatever we wanted. It could last a few hours or all day, but it was quality time and we still remember the specialness of it. Small things can make a big difference. There is a saying that sometime during your life you must spend time with your children – either when they're young, forming and training them, or later, visiting them in prison! As Maria Montessori says, "It's much easier to spend time forming the child than repairing the damaged adult".

Affirmation.

Conrad Baars, in his book, *Born Only Once*, deals with the "miracle" of affirmation, encouraging and expecting great things from people, whether they are spouses, children, employees or friends. People tend to live up to positive expectations of them. One of the best things to do for children is to affirm them, expect their best, and have confidence in them; this helps keep them in position for experiencing positive results in life. Negative expectations bring negative results, as found in a study of prisons in America, which revealed that 85% of all the inmates, while growing up or in their teens, had been told by their parents or other adults that they would never amount to anything, that they would wind up in prison and that their lives would be a failure! We parents (and priests!) should heed St. Paul's advice: "Say only the good things men need to hear, things that will really help them."

Approachability.
Being approachable is a necessity for both parents and priests. In 1961 Saint John XXIII wrote a letter to seminarians in which he emphasized the need for priests to be approachable so that people would feel comfortable about discussing their problems with them. This goes for parents, too. One of the saddest things I have experienced as a priest working with teens is the tearful distress in the voice of the pregnant girl who comes to me and says, "I could never tell my parents about this – they'd kill me." This is so sad because the problem could be safely dealt with if the parents showed their love for their kids by always being approachable. If children knew they could turn to their parents after making a mistake, to look forward to talking with them as with an understanding

and welcoming friend, things could be worked out and families saved from tragedy.

Accountability.

Children, growing up, need to know they are accountable to their parents, since it is the groundwork for all future social accountability. I've often found that in families where the parents' lives show they are accountable to God, the children have a sense of being accountable to their parents. If God is the overall, unseen presence in the home, if the parents are following the Ten Commandments and the laws of the Church, if they are striving to live prayerful Christian, Catholic lives, it is most likely that the children will acquire a taste for holiness and naturally assume the traits of obedience and accountability absorbed from the example given by their parents.

Authority.

The last A stands for authority, loving authority. This does not mean the authoritarian style of Captain von Trapp from

The Sound of Music before his change of heart. The children feared him because he ran his household like the strict Admiral on a battleship! Josh McDowell, a Christian counselor and author, talks about the four different types of parents: the Autocratic, Permissive, the Neglectful and the Relational. The Autocratic parents have lots of laws and rules but express no tenderness or love - the children on the battleship! The permissive parents are parents with love but who set no limits - the children are deprived of the opportunities for strengthening of character. The Neglectful ones are those who care little what the children do - there is no interested love and no limits. Lastly, there are the Relational parents, who have a loving relationship with their children and lay down certain guidelines. With regard to the goal of Excellence in Parenting, this last is the ideal balance to be achieved.

Josh McDowell has a great saying: "Rules without a relationship lead to rebellion". This applies to Family, Church or State. If parents give rules without having a relationship of love with their children, the children will tend to rebel against their parental authority. The same will happen in the Church. When people are lacking a real and faith-filled relationship with Christ which produces an attitude of loving obedience, they see only the structure and the organization and when expected to "follow the rules" they tend to rebel. One needs only to look out across the present day world-scene to see this same effect with governments. On the other hand, rules plus a relationship lead to response. We must have rules, but also genuine relationships of love in order to have responsive children. Of course, with parental authority comes the obligation to live a life of integrity and virtue to be worthy of the obedience that the children are expected to give.

I suggest parents read at least one good book a year on the subject of parenting, and observe other parents. If something effective is seen in what other parents do, forget the inhibitions and ask them for advice or suggestions. Parenting demands the balancing of love and limits. Some families are big on love and short on limits, while others may be just the opposite. It is necessary to find the proper balance that works with one's own temperament and the personalities and the uniqueness of the children. In order to do that it will help to apply the principle taught by St. Thomas Aquinas: "God's grace builds on nature." In the vocation of parenting, I believe working to create another Holy Family is achieved by developing natural qualities like these Twelve As and combining them with God's Ten Commandments; for the goal within the goal of Excellence in Parenting is, of course, not just having a happy, balanced family and home on earth, but getting both parents and children to their ultimate home in Heaven. In the field of parent-child relationships there are other wide and varied areas in which parent approachability alone would ease pain, build trust and solve problems. I'd like to suggest a few books helpful to parents. The first is *How to be a Hero to Your Kids,* by Josh McDowell, in which he talks about six

As of parenting. Another great book is *Raising Positive Kids in a Negative World* by Zig Ziglar. *Born Only Once*, by Conrad Baars and *The Key to Your Child's Heart* by Gary Smalley are also very good. The books of Maria Montessori: *The Secret of Childhood, The Absorbent Mind, The Child in the Church,* and *The Child in the Family* are excellent. Montessori was a devout Catholic and received many awards and praise for her work from the popes throughout this century. Spencer Johnson's The *One Minute Father* and the classic *How to Win Friends and Influence People* by Dale Carnegie are well worth reading, and *The Temperament God Gave You* by Art and Laraine Bennett is excellent. Lastly, I recommend a CD program by Brian Tracy and Barbara Young called *How to Raise Happy, Healthy, Self-Confident Children.*

III. Catholic Motherhood

A Mother's Prayer

Mother, take them over,

make them into Jesus,

form them in you as you formed him long

ago:

when a world went hating,

when *All Love* was waiting –

fold them in your waiting

as of long ago.

Mother take them over,

raise them into Jesus,

teach them all you taught your Son so long

ago:

when a world was yearning;

when a Boy was learning –

mold them in that learning

as of long ago.

Mother,

Form them into him,

mold them into him,

fashion them into your Only One!

Then Mother, give them over,

give them to the Father,

give them as you gave your Son so long ago -
-

when a world was crying,

when your Son hung dying –

hold them in that Dying

as of long ago!

Catholic Motherhood

The **M** in Motherhood stands for the **Mystery of Motherhood**. We find in scripture the words of St. Paul about Christian marriage being a mystery, in which a man will leave father and mother and cling to his wife, making the two one flesh (Eph 5:31). He says this is a great mystery referring to Christ and his Church. So the mystery of motherhood can be seen as an aspect of the Sacrament of Matrimony. The holy vocation of Matrimony is the calling of a man to leave father and mother and become one with his wife and is God's plan for bringing children into the world. Marriage, being a calling, is an authentic vocation, just as the priesthood or religious life is a vocation. It is God's personal invitation to a unique state of holiness. The great dignity of womanhood and motherhood is found in St. Paul's words about husbands and wives, who should love each other as Christ loved his Church (Eph 5:25). The husband symbolizes

Christ loving his Church; the woman symbolizes the Church loving Christ.

Since its beginning, the Church has always had a feminine identity, and has been known as the Bride of Christ and referred to as Holy Mother Church. It is the mystery of the feminine, of womanhood and motherhood.

In her vocation to holiness, woman as mother should remember that by her calling she personifies Holy Mother Church, the loving spouse of Christ; she participates in a real way in its mystery, imaging and reflecting in her personal life the Church as the bride of Christ and mother of his children.

Here are some parallel observations concerning motherhood and the mission of the Church. First of all, Holy Mother Church is the teacher; she governs her spiritual children and guides them through life to heaven. Mothers are the first teachers of children; they govern their growing years and guide them through earthly life. The Church provides a home for her children, feeds them with the Holy Eucharist; mothers make a home for children, feed and nourish them.

The Church cleanses and consoles in Confession, mothers bathe and soothe and wipe the eyes of hurting children. The Church, through the sacraments, strengthens and heals; Mothers bandage, nurse and comfort the members of her family. Oftentimes the Church will reconcile disparate and disagreeing children; mothers must often reconcile their disputing sons and daughters. But what is most important in this vocation of Mother is the interior awareness that she is ever a bride, giving first love to Christ, who loves her and his Church through her; and by letting the expression of that motherhood and all it means to become the aspiration to match the unconditional, selfless giving that Christ has shown her from the cross.

O is for **Openness to Life**. Once the marriage bond is established in the holy sacrament of Matrimony, there comes the awareness of the openness to new life, the possibility of a child. The Church has written beautifully about this. *Vatican II* says marriage and conjugal love are by their very nature ordained to the begetting and education of children. Children are really the supreme gift of marriage and contribute very substantially to the welfare of the parents. God himself wished to share with man a certain participation in his own creative work; thus he blessed male and female and gave the word and power to increase and multiply.

The Church has always linked, in its commentary on marriage, the beauty of openness to life with the Blessedness of Children: children are not to be thought of as burdens but as blessings. In Scripture they are gifts from God and parents are encouraged to be fruitful. Bishop Sheen called children "the incarnation of love". I often wonder how many parents ever think of it like this. When looking at their child, do they ever see the reality before them, the visible incarnation of the love they have and express for each other? Out of the physical expression of their love there actually came another person! That little child is their love personified!

There is another meditation for parents akin to this gift of life: it is the actual miracle of God's unseen infusion of a new and unique immortal soul into the incarnated sacred love of a husband and wife. They become co-creators and the wife becomes a shrine, a little church, a sanctuary. This is another similarity of the image of the Church and motherhood: the Church gives new birth to souls in Baptism, the woman gives birth to a new child in love. I am reminded of St. Anne, who could be called "The Sanctuary of the Immaculate Conception", because it was in her womb that God's supreme human being, Our Lady, was conceived. So the womb is truly a sanctuary, a sacred place, a place into which God himself infuses an immortal soul that will live forever. (It is interesting to note here that theologians have considered the question of when guardian angels are appointed to souls. The Church assures us that everyone has a guardian angel, but it has not been determined when this spiritual guardian enters into the life of a soul. Some theologians suggest it could happen at conception; others say at the time of birth. Some spiritual writers offer the thought that while the child is inside the mother the child is protected by the mother's guardian angel and takes over in the child's life upon separation from the mother's womb. Regardless, the answer is something that is definitely to be available in heaven!)

With regard to Openness to Life, seeing children as blessings from God, I encourage all parents to read the beautiful document *Humanae Vitae*, on the sanctity of human life.

We now come to **T** (not a pun!), the **Total Giving of Self**, the heart of sacrifice, the supreme quality implicit in the mystery of motherhood. This total donation of oneself is the heart of every valid vocation, but I think in marriage it might be the most humanly demanding and personally surrendering. The intimacy of husband and wife - now become father and mother - makes demands on them which require total self-submission to human and sacramental conditions not found in other vocations. With the close day to day family living, the stress of the workplace or tensions of health and temperament, parents are presented with unique situations for sacrifice and self-giving. For example: the yielding of opinion, the giving up of personal desire, the hiding of fatigue when child or spouse demands something more than one feels able (or willing!) to give - this is raw material for high sanctity and deep marital happiness. (Sometimes, when I think of the tired mother responding often through the night to the cry of a sick child - or of the father who takes over to give his wife the needed rest - I confess I thank God for rectories!)

H is for **The Heart of the Family**. Saint John Paul II has written about the daily heroism of mothers, of those brave mothers who devote themselves to their families without reserve, who are willing and ready to suffer for their children - making every effort and every sacrifice in order to pass on to them the best of themselves. The Pope says in living out their mission these stalwart women do not always find support in the world around them. On the contrary, the cultural models frequently promoted and broadcasted by the media do not encourage motherhood. In the name of progress, maternity and the values of fidelity, chastity and sacrifice - to which a host of Christian wives and mothers have carried and continue to bear outstanding witness - are presented as irrelevant and obsolete. And then the Pope addresses mothers this way: "We thank you heroic mothers for your invincible love. We thank you for your intrepid trust in God and in His love. We thank you for the sacrifice of your life; in the paschal mystery Christ restores to you the gift you gave him. Indeed he has the power to give you back the life you gave him as an offering." A beautiful passage from his encyclical, *the Gospel of Life.*

St. Paul speaks about the father as the spiritual head of the family and many spiritual writers have referred to the mother as the heart. The Church teaches that men and women, in their relationship with God, are equal but different; each has their own unique blessings, strengths, talents and gifts,

69

so fundamental for the necessary balance of family life and the character formation of children. St. Therese, who called herself "love in the heart of the Church", is a great example for mothers in the heart of the home. By their silent, contemplative, faithful presence, their warm encouragement and tender affection, by being good listeners and gentle admonishers - they truly are the heart of the home. The mother, as the heart of the family, should be the one to encourage prayer and to cooperate with the father in leading the children to God - to raise children for God, to form little saints. This also fosters the sanctity of the parents, whose vocation is to help each other to heaven along with the children. Their maintaining and encouraging of family prayer, with regular practices such as grace at meals, simple Bible readings, and the family rosary - if only a decade - creates an atmosphere of holiness which settles in the home and is absorbed by the children.

E is for **Evangelist**. In addition to spiritually forming the souls of her children, the mother must also be an evangelist, sharing the good news of the gospel with them. Evangelization is the extending of the gospel to everyone, everywhere, and who else but mothers can share the gospel message with children in a home? It is in the intimacy of the family setting, as the children grow and develop, that the Catholic Faith can be ideally passed on to future generations. The Church emphasizes the need for evangelizers and that the mother and father are the primary educators of children in the ways of faith. So the mother, the heart of the home, who has the direct attention of her children, must become their evangelizer, their personal teacher of the gospel.

Of course, in order to teach, the teacher must know the subject, and the way for a mother to teach the gospel to her children is first of all to learn it herself. Reading sacred scripture, studying the catechism, getting acquainted with the lives of the saints or listening to instructional CDs will support the decision to be a real evangelizer for the Church, with the calling to focus on the minds and hearts of children. Kimberly Hahn once said her way of changing the world was one diaper at a time! A great expression! She knew that she was having an impact upon society because she was educating her children, raising them in the faith, passing on the good news and laying the groundwork for future evangelizers who would find their role as priest, nun or dedicated lay person.

But being an evangelizer has a deeper dimension than that of teacher, and that is example. The mother must not only consider herself an evangelizer, but she must look like one. Christian example is the key to all successful evangelizing, and in the formative years of children's lives, it is more important than imparted knowledge: for example, to see a mother quietly praying or correcting in a gentle, patient tone has probably a greater effect on a child than listening to a gospel story!

R is for **Rewarding**. Motherhood is rewarding. So many mothers, including my own Mom and sister, have shared with me the great joys of motherhood, especially the unconditional love they receive from their children. "Who will ever love us as the child loves us?" said Maria Montessori, famous Catholic educator. The miracle of birth, the first step, the first word, the first drawing to stick on the refrigerator, the humorous things they say and do - all these and more mothers hold in their hearts as special, personal gifts. Dr. Montessori emphasizes the fact that every baptized child, clean of original sin - though subject to its effects - can be called a saint until the age of reason, until old enough to choose right from wrong. I think this is a mysterious and heaven-touched period in family life much overlooked by parents: the time when a sinless being, filled with the Christ-Life, moves among them and loves them. If parents were to seriously contemplate, in faith, the reality of this truth, they would find within themselves not only a tender respect for the purity and innocence of their young children, but also sacred opportunities for worshiping the Son of God in his Mystical Body as he gives himself into their care. There is a legend that an early Christian writer would go into his son's room

73

every night and kiss his forehead in honor and respect for the presence of God in his son's soul. He realized the great fact of the indwelling of the Blessed Trinity in the sinless soul of his young son.

Your reward will be great in heaven, Jesus said (Mt 5:12). He said whatever you did for the least of my brothers and sisters you did for me (Mt 25:40). I was hungry and thirsty and you gave me food and drink (Mt 25:35) - think of the meals a mother prepares for her children and the times she satisfies their thirst! The Lord also said in scripture the mere giving of a cup of water in his name will merit a reward (Mt 10:42).

I'm sure most mothers don't go through the day looking for a reward, but I hope they are aware that "love is its own reward", and since "God is Love", we could say that mothers - parents - are rewarded every day, since by the act of loving they participate in His very nature! That indeed is truly a foretaste of their eternal reward of being with God forever in heaven!

IV. Catholic Fatherhood

The Father

See how worried
your father and I have been
looking for you . . .
Did you not know
that I must be busy
with my Father's affairs?   ~ Luke 2:48, 49

With a hip-side bag of tools
and a boy hugged to his back –
joyfully apprenticed! –
Joseph had climbed the scaffold
of those childhood years;

now

atop these three last rungs of anxious days,
from this level Temple-high,
he views the rooftops of the past
and there,
ahead,
the distant ending of the road:

he knows the boy must now come down a man,

the boy who's found tools of his own
and new Apprenticeship:
this father's boy –

another Father's Son . . .

Turning to descend
he finds,
as ever was before,
a youngster's hand in his:
firmly,
like some set and heated brand,
he leaves the total impress
of all he ever owned
of fatherhood.

Catholic Fatherhood

I once heard Father Robert Fox tell a story about unwittingly going above the speed limit on his way to give a lecture. When pulled over by a police officer, Father explained that he was the featured speaker for the program and that he was running late. "My name is Father Fox," he offered. "Listen," the state trooper retorted, "I don't care if you're Mother Goose, you still get the ticket!"

Of course, the title of "Father" does not give anyone exemption from the penalties for breaking the law. But being a father - in the ordinary sense - does bring with it both serious responsibilities and incomparable joy. God calls fathers to be the spiritual leaders of their families. Saint John Paul II said in his Apostolic Exhortation *Familiaris Consortio* that through their vocation as husbands and fathers, men are called to show the importance of rebuilding society. Contrary to the prevailing secular view that fathers are

77

superfluous (argued blatantly in an article published by the American Psychological Association), the Pope insists that fathers are irreplaceable and utterly important. Here are seven key principles of fatherhood that I link to the word "**FATHERS.**"

Faithful.

To be faithful means, first of all, to be full of *Faith*, the theological virtue given to us in baptism. Fathers are called to develop this virtue like a seed planted in the heart and nurtured through the exercise of prayer, the sacraments, spiritual reading, study and reflection, and obedience. Next, faithfulness means to be committed to one's vocation, to be spiritually trustworthy and persevering in one's calling: the husband and father is called to practice fidelity to his promises, his covenants, the vows he made in marriage and in the family, willingly fulfilling all the duties of his state of life. Finally, fathers are to practice faithfulness in the workplace, being a dedicated employee or employer in whatever field providence has arranged. In short, God calls fathers to faithfulness, first in professing the Catholic Faith and second in living the Christian life. For Catholics, this can be further defined as being obedient to the teachings of the Church, the Holy Father, and the directives of the Magisterium.

Apostolic.

Each father is called to have an apostolic dimension to his life, a desire to reach out to others beyond the family, to share and spread the Faith, to help to bring souls closer to God. Father Faber once said, "If you don't try to convert the world, the world will convert you." Precisely. If we don't actively try to bring the world *to* Christ, the world will take us *away* from Christ. According to Vatican II, every baptized Catholic has the obligation to spread the Catholic Faith and is given the strength to do so by Confirmation. But I believe fathers are uniquely gifted to extend the fatherhood of God by participating in the missionary work of the Church.

I think the Catholic father, besides helping to get his wife and children to heaven, should be conscious of a wider responsibility to share the Catholic Faith with others. The Holy Father, in a document on the family, says fathers are called to evangelize other fathers, mothers other mothers, and children other children. Children sometimes have a bit of trouble understanding this. I once gave a talk to a grade-school class telling how I used to evangelize with the Legion of Mary, setting up a pamphlet rack on a busy street corner and giving out free Catholic literature to passers-by. "This was *evangelizing*," I said. One wide-eyed student raised his hand and said, "Father, didn't you get in trouble for *vandalizing* on street corners?" But even children can understand that we are all called to reach out to people like ourselves. The Pope calls this the apostolate of like-unto-like, and it is the way society will be saved. Catholic fathers, then, are called to be concerned about the salvation of their neighbours, relatives, and friends who are unchurched or have left the practice of the Catholic Faith. In the Church today, the Holy Spirit has made available several organizations and movements that a Catholic father can consider joining. It is possible for fathers with even small children to be active in the Church. For example, I know of families with several small children where both parents are in the Legion of Mary. They attend meetings on different nights, thereby enabling each to be involved in the apostolic life of the Church.

Another way to be apostolic is to be an example at work, witnessing to the Christian life by being a genuine, honest, conscientious Catholic presence to co-workers. One of the best evangelizers I know is a hairdresser who keeps a little picture of Jesus on a mirror. When her customers say something like, "Oh, that's a nice picture," she proceeds to talk to them about God, prayer, or some aspect of the Catholic faith. Of course, with those sharp scissors snipping close to the ears, she holds their attention well!

Tender-hearted.

Being tender-hearted does not mean being weak or leaning toward the feminine; it means being patient and gentle toward one's spouse and children. This virtue requires self-control, discipline, and humility. Tenderness is a strength, not a weakness - being strong enough to be affectionate towards one's spouse and children. And being tender has tangible benefits. Zig Ziglar tells about a German insurance company that did a fifty-year study of all their employees. They found that if the husband had an affectionate, tender relationship with his wife, he lived an average of five years longer and had a much larger income than husbands with a less affectionate relationship!

The same principle applies to children, and I repeat here for fathers what was recommended above: give the kids at least twelve hugs a day, the breakdown being three hugs for securing survival, six to promote emotional well being, and twelve to establish emotional growth. Being tender expresses respect for the dignity and beauty of the other person; it shows appreciation for these things with genuine, unashamed affection. Tenderness is akin to meekness, another misunderstood word. One definition of meekness is: "to be not easily provoked." In a father's relationship with wife or children, quiet, gentle patience gives them the experience of a calm and tender love and is a support for the psychological security every family needs. In *Familiaris Consortio*, the Holy Father calls on each husband to have a profound respect for the dignity of his wife, manifesting his love for her with a charity that is both gentle and strong, such as Christ has for the Church. Society is ultimately influenced for the better by the family whose head is like Christ in his expressions of love.

Holiness.

Every Catholic father is called to live a life of sanctity. It's not only priests and nuns who are called to sanctity: It is a universal vocation applying to every man, woman, and child. A priest once noted, "It's one thing to be a good father; it's another thing to be a holy father." Even an atheist can be a good husband, being nice to his wife, but he cannot be a holy husband. The Christian father is called to realize that marriage is a vocation to holiness - that *his expression of his love for wife and children is to be the expression of his love for God.*

With every vocation comes the grace to achieve its fulfilment, and for the Christian father, the first step is prayer. He must not leave it up to his wife to do all the praying; he must become a man of prayer himself. One way of developing an interior life of prayer is to set aside some specific prayer time every day - twenty minutes, half of an hour, perhaps a visit to the Blessed Sacrament after work. Other good disciplines are the habit of daily Mass, and night prayer with the family. Since God is holy, conversation with Him is the first step. As fuel for your prayer life, it is imperative to select good spiritual reading like the Lives of the Saints and Sacred Scripture and allow some time for reading each day. Get good

84

Catholic periodicals come into the home. Or try what I call spiritual listening, listening to recordings of books and talks in the car while sitting in traffic or on break time at the job. There are many excellent CDs available by spiritual leaders such as Bishop Sheen and Scott Hahn, and complete books like the Bible, Imitation of Christ, etc. (Before the advent of the CD, when only tapes were available, I would remind people to be not only "bookworms"; but also "tapeworms"!) This can all be summed up in what is called a *rule of life*. The phrase means setting up a spiritual routine, certain things you do each day, each week. A rule of life is custom-made for each person: it needn't be a long list of things but just enough to keep discipline and order in the spiritual life - set times for prayer, spiritual reading, regular confession, etc. As a father, make sure that every year you read at least one book on parenting and one book on spousal relationships to stroke your interest in being a good father, out of love for God and family. In addition, making a retreat once a year, or at least taking an

85

occasional day of recollection, should also be part of a father's program of self-betterment for the sake of himself and his family.

A father's spiritual life has an enormous effect on the rest of the family, and that's why it should come first. This is not selfish but is almost obligatory if the father is to be the head of the family. Consider an illustration: on a jet flight, if the plane loses cabin pressure, the flight attendant instructs you to put your own mask on first and *then* to help your children with theirs. It doesn't say take care of your kids' masks first and then, if there's still enough air, take care of yourself. A father's focus on his own relationship with God, on his own prayer life and spiritual well-being, actually benefits his wife and children. Breathing the pure air of sanctity ensures that the father will be able to help his family on all the levels of their earthly existence, and especially in their heavenly one.

Educator.

86

Papal documents say that every father is called to be committed to the education of his children. One of the purposes of marriage, as Vatican II emphasized, is the procreation and *education* of children. How is a father an educator of his children? First, just by being a father: Every moment he is teaching them by his actions, words, and example. There is a saying that example speaks so loud, we can't hear what the person says.

In my former parish, there was a nun whose brother was a priest. Both were inspired to enter religious life by their father, a very simple man. Each day before going out to work on the ranch, he would come down the steps, kneel at a special spot in the living room, and say his morning prayers. Those little kids saw their dad kneeling in prayer, oblivious of his surroundings, and this helped foster their religious vocations. Don't *push* people, goes the old maxim, for they will fall in that direction. What a father wants to do is *pull*: And children are pulled towards Christ by watching how their parents live their daily lives.

Reflection.

Fathers are called to be a reflection of God, the original Father. Saint John Paul II says fathers reveal and relive on earth the very fatherhood of God. What constitutes fatherhood? The giving of life. In the creed, we say we believe in "one God the Father the Almighty, maker of heaven and earth, of all things visible and invisible". God is a father because he begets his Son, the eternal Son of God, "eternally begotten of the Father" (Ephesians 3:15). The Old Testament Jews did not really understand the fatherhood of God; God was their creator and their Lord. It was not until Jesus came and made known to them that God was "ABBA," the Aramaic word for *"Daddy"*.

It should be awe-inspiring for a father to realize his children will get their image of God from his own human fatherhood. If a father is harsh, stern, distant, and uncaring, his children will most likely tend to see God in the same way. If a father is tender, loving, merciful, and forgiving, then his children will have a much easier time seeing a true reflection of God. As they learn to pray the "Our Father," one of these two images will present itself to them and mold their spiritual outlook. Of course, we know that God's grace can compensate for a father's human weaknesses, and that He is able to heal the damaged vision of a child who's been deprived of a loving and gentle image of Him. Nevertheless, fathers must realize the responsibility that is theirs – that they are reflections of God the Father in the lives of their children and that they must work at being God-like, at discovering the Father-heart of God.

St. Joseph.

The man God chose for the role of father to his own Son was the most perfect reflection of the fatherhood of God. He was God's earthly counterpart, the true template of a Christian father's life. All fathers and husbands are called to take St. Joseph as model, guide, and inspiration; to imitate the prayer and holiness of the obedient one who followed the will of God in his life without questioning.

St. Joseph was no less than Jesus' own role model - the reflection of God the Father for God's own Son as he was growing up! Today, too, fathers should find their model in Joseph the provider, Joseph the protector, Joseph the worker, Joseph the husband and father. He was the least holy of the Holy Family, but still he was its head. Many fathers will relate to that, as they become aware and are moved by the innocence and beauty they discover in their children and wives. Responsible unworthiness - it's a mysterious trait of the Catholic father. It is sustained by adapting St. Joseph's practice of living in the presence of God. To be exposed to the sun is to be tanned by its rays; to be a reflection of God the Father, fathers must live in that brilliance, humbly accepting their weaknesses along with the graces of responsibility, offering all they are and do to God the Father of all. Then they will become:

Faithful fathers, solid in commitment to God, spouse, and children.

Apostolic fathers reaching out to other dads and bringing them closer to the Church.

Tender-hearted fathers, gentle, loving and welcoming in family life.

Holy fathers, called to be channels of sanctity for friends and family.

Educators of their families in the Catholic Faith.

Reflectors of God, mirrors of the all-caring, all-giving Father.

St. Joseph-style fathers, making him their model and companion on the sacred journey toward true Catholic fatherhood.

V. St Joseph and Fatherhood

The Fatherhood of Joseph

Joseph was a young man,
Joseph was in love,
and the maiden's name was Mary
he was thinking of.

Joseph was a husband,
Joseph loved a wife:
he gave himself to Mary --
gave himself for life.

Joseph was protector
of God's home on earth,
parent and provider
for Mary's Child from birth.

Joseph was a father
to God's only Son:
of all mankind created
Joseph was the one,

and Joseph's still protector
of God's home on earth --
Joseph who's been father

to Jesus since his birth --
And now we all are Jesus,
in him we are one:
Joseph is our father,
we are Joseph's Son!

St. Joseph and Fatherhood

Every person has a vocation - the universal call to sanctity - and some questions to be asked are: "Am I responding to the call to holiness? Am I growing in virtue? Do I seek to be Christ-like?" And for husbands and fathers I suggest the question, "Am I following the example of St. Joseph?" Here are a few reflections on the life and example of St. Joseph, the patron and model for all husbands and fathers, using his name as a guide.

J - Joseph the Just Man.

Sacred Scripture and Saint John Paul II (in his apostolic exhortation *The Guardian of the Redeemer*) refer to Joseph as the *Just* man, meaning that he was a holy man, a righteous man, a man of honesty, integrity, and virtue. St. Joseph is the greatest saint and holiest human person after the Blessed Mother. In fact, some of the Doctors of the Church claim that there was no grace ever given to any of the saints that was not given to St. Joseph as well.

94

St. Thomas Aquinas says that God gives grace proportionate to our office and to our state in life. So if you are a husband and father, you will be given the grace to be a holy husband and father. If someone is ordained a priest, he will be given the grace to be a holy priest. Think how much grace St. Joseph received to be the foster father of the Son of God and the virginal spouse of Mary, the Immaculate Conception. St. Joseph is the greatest of saints because he was the closest one to Jesus and to the Blessed Mother.

O - Joseph the Obedient one.

Joseph was truly obedient to the will of God in his life. The Angel said, "Have no fear about taking Mary as your wife," and as soon as Joseph knew God's will for him, he obeyed. When the angel told Joseph that Herod was planning to destroy the child, Joseph responded immediately and began the flight to Egypt.

Some people ask if St. Joseph was old. This is due to the apocryphal writings of the early Church, ancient writings which were not divinely inspired, or approved by the Church as Sacred Scripture. One such writing says that when Joseph married the Blessed Mother he was eighty-nine years old, and that he died at the age of one hundred and eleven! There is nothing in the Bible regarding the age of St. Joseph. We can be assured that Mary did not have to push her aged husband in a wheelchair across the desert! There is a tradition that he was young and strong, perhaps in his thirties. Common sense tells us that he would have had to be physically in shape to manage the journey to Egypt and back, and to work as a carpenter during the years Jesus was growing up. He was Our Lady's guardian and protector. Scripture speaks about Mary's betrothal to a "man" named Joseph. It does not use the word for an "old man", as it does for Simeon or Zachary. Even in the ancient catacomb of Priscilla, Joseph was pictured as a young man without a beard!

Joseph was an obedient man who never questioned Divine Providence. Even though Mary was more than eight months pregnant, Joseph believed it was God's will for them to leave Nazareth and go down to Bethlehem. This was to fulfil the prophecy of Micah (scripture with which Joseph was familiar) that the Savior would be born in Bethlehem. Joseph abandoned himself to the will of God, and today, when a father asks himself, "Am I obedient to the will of God? Am I obedient to the Ten Commandments, to the teaching of Christ and the Church on marriage and family life?" he should "Go to St. Joseph" in prayer, a providential friend and confidante of husbands and fathers.

S - Joseph the Silent One.

Surprisingly, there are no recorded words of St. Joseph in Scripture. There are words in the Old Testament for the other Joseph - the great Patriarch - that the Church has applied to St. Joseph, but no spoken words of his are found in the New Testament. Yet his silent presence is like a dominant voice. Even his death is wrapped in silence; there is no account as to when he died or where he was buried. He was a man of deep interior life, who kept in touch with the silent centre of his being. A habit of interior solitude and silence helps develop a true life of prayer, and Joseph was a man of prayer who listened to the *Word of God* who had actually become his foster son! External things did not distract him - he was a man conscious of the internal, unseen life of the God-indwelling soul.

We picture St. Joseph as a silent worker, as a craftsman, who endured and suffered in silence. He was not a complainer and did not show anger with God by saying, "Why are you doing this, why must we flee to Egypt?" He was a man of patience, who accepted the events of daily life in silent willingness. To emulate St. Joseph, a father could ask himself: "Do I have enough silence in my life? Do I spend quiet time with my family and enough time in prayer with Jesus? Do I listen to Jesus when he speaks to me in the Sunday readings? Do I spend time before the Blessed Sacrament listening to Jesus who is truly present as he was truly present in the house of Joseph? Do I waste my speech with empty words, or worse - am I critical or judgmental in my speech about others?"

E - Joseph the Example.

Imagine the kind of man Joseph was. God the Father chose him out of the whole human race to be the man to raise his only begotten Son, Jesus Christ. When a baby sitter is needed, not just anyone is picked, even if it is for only a few hours. The all-knowing God chose St. Joseph to be the model for His Son in his early years of human life. He was an example to Jesus in word and action and a true father to him in every way except for physical generation. He was the father who taught Jesus how to speak, how to read, and how to make doors and plows. Remember the saying, "Your example is so loud I can't hear what you're saying!" Joseph was the perfect example for the Christ Child, the mold of his manhood.

Joseph and Mary home schooled
Jesus. Though he was the Son of God and
had the Beatific Vision, Jesus had to grow in
experiential knowledge and had to develop
into maturity. He looked up to St. Joseph as
every child does its father, imitating his
mannerisms. A father's reflection could be:
"What kind of example do I give my wife
and children? Am I living out the vocation as
spiritual leader of my family? Can I do more
to teach the kids the Faith? Do I do enough
to keep up with my own Faith, like making
time for spiritual reading or listening to
uplifting CDs or getting to a retreat during
the year?"

P - Joseph the Patron.
Joseph is the Patron Saint of husbands,
fathers and workers. There should be a place
for him in every man's life regardless of the
"lifestyle". For husbands and fathers, there
should be a statue or picture of him in every
home, so children could get to know about
him, and the head of the family be reminded
100

of the challenge to adopt his example. His feast days should be noted and celebrated.

He is also the Patron Saint of the Universal Church. Everything that St. Joseph did for Jesus he now does for the Church. Why? Because the Catholic Church is the Mystical Body of Christ. The Blessed Mother is the mother of the Church and St. Joseph is the foster father and guardian of the Church. He is also the Patron Saint of a happy death, which means dying in the arms of Jesus and Mary and in the embrace of Holy Mother Church. A Father's prayers to St. Joseph should invoke his intercession through his titles: for himself as a father and husband, for his family, for his work and for his Church; and he might want to include this prayer as well:

The Hail Joseph

Hail Joseph,

Man of faith,

The Lord is with you;

Blessed is your wife among virgins

And blessed is the fruit of her womb, Jesus.

Holy Joseph,

Father to God,

Pray for your children now

And at the hour of our death, Amen.

H - St. Joseph, Helper of the Blessed Mother.

St. Joseph was the virginal spouse of the Blessed Virgin Mary. In God's plan of salvation, he was a loving husband, kind, considerate, affectionate, and self-sacrificing. St. Joseph had the responsibility for spiritual leadership as the head of the Holy Family. God's messages from the angel were revealed to *him*, even though he was chosen as the head of that family, just as every father is the spiritual head of his own family; the Blessed Mother was far holier than he, due to her Immaculate Conception. St. Joseph couldn't help being conscious of his utter humanness, living with a wife free of Original Sin and a Son who was Divine! Yet he knew that he was called to help, to assist in raising his very God now existing as a human child, and that special woman called to the high destiny of Divine Motherhood.

This is the state of humility that should be the aspiration of all Christian parents, for just as there is the Mystical Body of Christ there is the Mystical Home of Nazareth, where the Holy Family continues to live, in a mystical but real way, through the faithful Catholic Family.

They help, guide and sustain each other, making a home - as only a father and mother could - for that same silent Presence that shines out at them from an innocent child's eyes: the infinite, all-powerful God now subject and limited to the restricted human condition - once confined to Nazareth

- now continuing on through the centuries in the Catholic Church.

VI. Shaping the Soul of a Child

A Parent's Prayer

Mary,

Give us your eyes,

When the light has left our skies,

When there seems no sun to rise --

When being cries to see –

Before faith dies,

Give us your eyes.

Mary,

Give us your smile,

When the distant storm clouds pile,

When hope goes its lonely mile

With only trial to see –

This little while,

Give us your smile

Mary,

Give us your song,

When the days go dark or wrong,

When the heart has laboured long

And may no longer see –

Give us your eyes,

Your smile,

Your song –

Let love be strong.

Shaping the Soul of a Child

The role of parents - and grandparents - when it comes to the personal development of children, is a demanding, multifaceted one. Prolonging their innocence, protecting their integrity, guiding their knowledge, etc. - all have a seriousness of their own; but when it comes to what is most important for children in the Catholic family, living with the many treasures and graces of the One True Faith, *shaping the soul of a child must be primary.* Children must be taught how to live the life of Heaven, their ultimate, God-intended destination. This should be the ultimate focus for parents: to become saints themselves, and raise their children to sanctity. **S** is the first letter in the word **Shaping** and it stands for **Sanctity**. For all humankind in general, and for Catholic parents in particular, the supreme goal in life should be to become a saint. This is far from pious admonition but is in fact the ultimate necessity! The best thing parents can do for their kids is to become closer to God themselves. As with the example of the

107

cabin pressure changes on a plane - the putting on of your own mask first and then the child's, is a very important bit of information! If parents are faithful to this aspect of their marital state, the whole family will know growth in holiness. One caution: there needs to be spiritual freedom for each member of the family - especially children - for the Holy Spirit to act within them. Rigidly structured devotions or insisted practices will prohibit the intended effects of Grace. Holiness for children is *attracted,* not *extracted.* Example is powerful. The rule is "Gently Pull, not Roughly Push." A home with genuine prayer and a sense for the need for holiness eases everyone along the way; imposed devotions can often cause traffic jams!

The second letter is **H**, for **Honor**. Honor, respect, reverence for the dignity of the child. Honor is the basis of all Ten Commandments: *Honor* the Lord's Day, *Honor* the Lord's Name, *Honor* Your Parents, *Honor* the Sanctity of Life, *Honor* the Sanctity of Marriage, *Honor* the Sanctity

of Other People's Property, *Honor* Truth.
There is no happy marriage, no happy family
if this basic quality of honor, this
interchanging respect for husband, wife and
children, is missing in the home. In the
writings of Saint John Paul II honor is a
central and recurring theme; honor of and for
the human person, especially the dignity of
children, made in God's image and likeness.
We have the Lord's own word that unless we
change and become like little children we
cannot enter the kingdom of God! (Mt 18:3).
Reading and meditating on the ineffable
dignity of the Holy Family can assure
Catholic parents of the security of not falling
away from the ideals of their calling. Along
with the writings of Saint John Paul II, I
would recommend books by Maria
Montessori, the Catholic educator and
teacher, especially *The Secret of Childhood*.
A genuine sense of the dignity of children
and the honor that is due them can be found
in her writings; she shows how "the Child"
builds the adult, and how much respect - and
even gratitude - is due to the Child in general

and even to the Child each of us once was!
Here is an insight into Montessori's
understanding of the dignity of "the Child":

I Am the Child

I am the Child,
I am the one who made your mind
before you came to know,
The one who built your being
in the time before you had to go –
You couldn't know
What need you had of me.

I am the Child,
With hands of mine you worked your world
until it came to be,
And through my eyes you saw things
things that stirred your yearning to be free –
You couldn't see
The need you had of me.

I was your teacher then,

Your guide from day to day;

And I remember when you left me

110

As you sought your way:

I am the Child,
I am the one whose cry you'll hear
in every child to be,
To all your hopes, to all your dreams,
I have been your one forgotten key!
Oh you must see
You once had need of me –
You still have need of me –
Oh will you ever see
What need you have
Of me!

The letter **A** is for the **Apostolate***;*
children should be acquainted with the sense
of sharing the Catholic Faith with others, to
become apostles. It is by sharing and
professing the Faith that they will secure it,
and it is one way to protect them from being

influenced by the secular and pagan environment they experience now, and will continue to face as they grow older. It has been my observation that "unevangelizing" Catholics are usually the ones "evangelized" by other religions. If kids become active in appreciating and spreading their faith as children, they will most likely be much more committed to keeping their faith as adults. Though children are kept busy with school and athletic activities, to keep the mission of sanctifying them in focus it is most important for parents to involve them in *service* of some kind, some spiritual formation program that would include visiting a nursing home, helping the homebound, doing errands for neighborhood shut-ins, etc. In the parish there may be youth groups or organizations like the Junior Legion of Mary to consider. But however done, the time, effort and ingenuity it will take to fit evangelizing activity into busy family life must have the one intention of developing the spiritual and apostolic life of the children; but it will also be actual, sanctifying experience for the parents. And it helps maintain a presence of the *spiritual* in the dominant flow of natural life. It is a spiritual principle to *link an action to a doctrine;* for example, when visiting the sick or shut-ins, the kids would be told they are visiting not only those persons but also Jesus, who is present in them by his having taken on a human existence. If the kids are taught how to make rosaries, they should be taught the history of the rosary, how to say it, why it is said, etc. Then they should be encouraged to give them out to others, along with their own explanation. Things like this will not only help a great deal in keeping children Catholic, but will hold the family in the security of Grace-filled living.

Protect is the word for **P**; protect your children's purity; safeguard their innocence. Protect from whom? Safeguard from what? The Bible and the Church tell us plainly: *The World, the Flesh, and the Devil.* Today it is a daunting challenge to be a protector of innocent youth, in a neo-pagan culture where Christianity is targeted for annihilation. We no longer have "Christendom" to support our moral values. Today, God-fearing people live in a walled-in world, surrounded by heights of secularism, humanism, atheism; they are forced to see offensive sights and listen to lust-filled lies through the daily onslaught of the anti-Christian multi-media. What can parents do, living in a world like this? We must do what we can to refute the great accusations and falsehoods that come upon us, but I think the answer is found in "God's multimedia", the Bible and the Catholic Church. We are told to be *in the world but not of the world; that the world will hate us because it hated him; that he has overcome the world.* Because of the vast, out-of-control moral disorder we see around us, I think it urgent that the meaning of these words, somehow, must be passed on to our children, regardless of age and allowing for their level of understanding. Tell them openly what the world is, where we stand as Christians and Catholics; let them hear, and hear repeatedly, that evil is overcome by holiness and trust in the *world*

114

we do not see, the real world of faith; by being good Catholics, that Christ lives on in us, that our purpose for *being* here is to get ready to *leave* here, to do all we can to *spiritualize* their minds and leave the results in the hands of Mary, Mother of Divine Providence. We are told it will be given us what to say when we face crucial times; I believe this is one of those times. It is in the world that we are sanctified - but sanctified *in union with Christ*, who has overcome this world.

As regards the Flesh, the perversion of sexuality as independent from marriage and accepted as a social entertainment or personalized pleasure has deprived many children of their innocence and their actual childhood. Today all parents are witnesses to the prevalence and availability of sexual knowledge through various media and technological advances, and it seems impossible to keep it from children. You would almost have to presume that, after a certain age - and now that age can be very young - the child has already acquired sexual

115

knowledge that would have been unheard of
not so very long ago! What I have suggested
to parents is to have sincere and direct but
guarded conversations with the children
individually, sensitively determining the
extent of their knowledge and assuring them
of your genuine acceptance of them and your
unconditional love and companionship,
humbly asking to be consulted whenever and
with whatever they may want to bring up. As
with all family challenges, prayer and some
personal sacrifices for the grace to accept and
endure the situation is very much advised.
As for the Devil, children should know that
the devil and demons are real and cause or
influence evil in the world, but this
knowledge must be tailored to the age and
make-up of the individual child and should
be taught in the beautiful light of creation and
God's protective love for us. Evil and the
existence of the devil should be given its
actual place in the child's creed, without
diminishment or exaggeration; this will give
the child the proportion of importance evil
has within the full scope of the spiritual life,

which can be lived without reference to it or its detrimental influence.

An obvious yet most important duty in the job of protecting children from the evils of the age is another P, which I suggest stands for *promotion,* the promotion of Christian values and culture. To promote good music, genuinely beautiful art; good literature, wholesome movies and DVDs were the basic recommendations from most of the moms in my parish when asked what they do. Favorites were C. S. Lewis' The *Chronicles of Narnia* and the writings of Tolkien's *The Hobbit* and *The Lord of the Rings* which Tolkien - a devout Catholic - said was definitely a Catholic book that contains many Christian and Catholic themes. Of course, first and foremost, they mentioned a good children's Bible; along with the lives of the saints; both are available in versions for all ages and can be had on DVD. Most religious stores stock these and of course there is always the internet!

The **I** in **Shaping** stands for **Influences,** the bad and the good. Some time ago I came across an interesting study that I use to compare what influenced kids in the1950s with what influences kids today. Back in the 50s the number one influence on children was *parents and family*; number two was *the school* (almost every parish had a school); *the Church* was number three (the closeness to priests in thriving parishes, the relationship with teaching Sisters, the cohesiveness of Catholic doctrine and liturgy); number four was *friends,* and number five was *the media*. In a recent study the number one influence on kids today is *their friends*. That's why it is so important to know the friends of the kids, who they hang around with, and how much time and effort they put into those friendships. *The Media* is now number two up from number five! This is so easy to understand, with the obvious dominance of movies, TV, music and personality cults all around them. *Parents and family* are down to number three, *the school and teachers* down to number four.

118

And number five: *their church, their parish.* What are parents to do? How to get back again from number three to being number one? In this connection I refer you to the above articles on Motherhood and Fatherhood in which I explore the needs of children that only the parents can fill: the selfless building of a real relationship by spending more time with the kids, giving the necessary hugs, etc. I know from pastoral experience that these things are not only beneficial but in today's world are absolutely necessary for interacting love to survive. I have also considered previously the importance of passing on the Faith to the kids by parents and grandparents, but what about godparents? They also should be involved in this shaping of the child's soul. They should be encouraged to pray every day for their godchildren and to try to include them in their own lives by some means of personal connection - a religious card or gift on the anniversary of their Baptism and the other sacraments. They should be invited if possible to family events, or arrangements could be made for the kids to spend some time through the year with their godparents, keeping in mind the value of good influence from whatever source possible. Parents could arrange to get other families of good influence to be part of their lives, so that the opportunities will increase for the kids to be exposed to the genuine goodness in others; which will help to offset the influence of the pop culture and secular environment.

The last two letters in **Shaping** are **N** for **Nature** and **G** for **Grace**. The maxim of Saint Thomas Aquinas - *grace builds on nature* - is a necessary principle for parents to follow. What can be done in the natural order to help children become saints? To help them realize their integrity and their dignity as children of God? Fundamentally this begins with the acquiring of *good habits*. Remember, good habits are hard to form but easy to live with; they make life better! Bad habits are easy to form but hard to live with; they make life miserable! Good habits - or rather *habits for good,* especially those of order - which are built upon natural living

120

experiences, such as finishing an action (regularly making one's own bed, closing opened drawers, clicking off turned-on lights, etc.) become natural bases for the inner habits of spiritual awareness and prayer as children develop in the dimension of grace. They are the foundation for the forming of the natural virtues: kindness, generosity, unselfishness and self-discipline.

It is important to work at forming these qualities in children early. It is common knowledge that self-discipline - doing what you should do and when you should do it, whether you feel like it or not - is the root of success in every field. Children should be taught as early as possible to develop the natural virtues of generosity, cooperation, obedience, responsibility, forgiveness, respect, etc., for these are the necessary foundation needed by the Lord to build his supernatural virtues upon them. (One element to be supplied by the parents in all this is an effort to make the home a place of peace, love, and genuine joy. Grace thrives where nature is at peace, and to strive for a tranquil home is a major component for the successful perfecting of the child's natural and spiritual life.)

Grace is the interacting and overseeing influence in one's spiritual life, the gift of God that enables a human being to participate in the life of Christ, which continues in history through the sacraments of the Catholic Church. This grounding of the natural virtues in children is intended to become the seedbed for the supernatural virtues of faith, hope, and charity, prudence, justice, temperance and fortitude. These are the Big Ones, the ones that come with the Lifetime Guarantee! When dealing with parenting and God's grace, the fundamental thing for parents to do is to pray for their children. Where does grace come from? How does it reach your child? It comes through prayer! Parents tell me often that when it comes to parenting, everything depends on grace. And where do they get their grace? From prayer and the sacraments. I always insist that they pray every day for their children, and make them a special

122

intention at every Mass and Communion. They should realize they are praying not merely for the natural welfare of the children, but for the maturing of their spiritual life, where they will be filled with Sanctifying Grace, the personal indwelling of the Blessed Trinity, the sharing in the great mystery of eternal life which has already begun in their own practicing Catholic lives.

And lastly under Grace comes not only praying for the child and their link to the sacraments, but making use of the sacramentals of the Faith. This could include the Enthronement of the Sacred Heart of Jesus in the home, or the seasonal sacramentals that can be explained or discussed as they come up throughout the year, like the Advent Wreath and Jesse Tree, the Lenten ashes, the palm at Eastertide; personal rosaries and miraculous medals for each member of the family; devotional candles to light before the statue of Our Lady in May or October, and the daily availability of Holy Water. A small holy water font at the front or back door will develop the good habit of blessing one's self, and I recommend blessing the children's rooms with holy water when, for example, teens are out for the evening, or occasionally in the kitchen or den - where the family most often gathers. You'll notice a difference.

Parents should do all they possibly can to keep their children connected to the sacraments. Regarding Baptism, it should be done as early as possible, for this is the birth of the child into the life of grace. Waiting to perform Baptism delays the child's soul from participating in the actual life of Christ, and could open it to an undesirable influence from the very real spirit world. For First Confession and onward, help is needed to form the conscience of children, the first basic lesson being to learn what is right and what is wrong. Walk them through the Ten Commandments and guide them through an examination of conscience. Once they make their first confession, take them to confession regularly, especially when they're teenagers! They may not want to go, but something like, *"This is our monthly family confession; we all go together,"* might be used. Parents tell me they notice that often after family confession the kids are more helpful and agreeable around the house! Frequent reception of the Eucharist is, of course, the natural (and supernatural!) complement to confession. Remember, it's all a matter of grace, getting as much grace into the life of a child as possible. In preparation for Confirmation help them to pick the name of a saint they can emulate and have as a role model. A biography of the saint, a patron saint medal or statue are "grace-full" gifts for this occasion. Confirmation can be a powerful, transforming sacrament in the lives of teens. With regard to every sacrament, as with the Catholic religion itself, it is what *is unseen that is the most important!* Teach the kids that real miracles and inner, invisible realities are what the Catholic Faith is all about. I recall a beautiful quote from St. Augustine: *"Faith is to believe in what we don't see; the reward for that faith is to see what we believe."* For example, at Baptism we see the pouring of water; invisibly what is happening is a spiritual birth of the child who has become "the Flesh of Christ" as St. Basil writes. In Confession we face a priest, but the sacramental reality is the actual presence of Christ before us; we hear the flow of the words of absolution in our ears, but faith tells us they are the mystical Blood of Christ washing sin from the soul. In the Eucharist, kids should be told that the bread and wine they see after the consecration is the actual Real Presence of the Lord; it may look like bread and smell like wine but is not so any more! Their "faith-eyes" have witnessed a miracle - Christ is there, Body, Blood, Soul and Divinity. If we can get our Catholic children, who must ultimately face the unavoidable reality of sin, to be aware of or actually realize the unseen realities revealed by God in their Catholic Faith, they will always be on the road to goodness, moral safety and perhaps to real sanctity at the end. Give them the rhyme I learned growing up from an old holy pastor: *Do your best and let God do the rest!*

VII. Teaching Mary to Children

A Child's Prayer to Mary

Mother of God's little Child,

I am little too;

Guide my steps and clear my path,

lead me home to you;

for you're my mother too,

I depend on you,

I am little

like your little Child.

Mother of God's precious Child,

I am precious too;

he grew up and died for me

and he gave me you:

You're my mother too,

I belong to you,

I am precious

like your precious Child.

Mother of God's holy Child,

make me holy too;

keep my heart from every wrong,

keep it close to you:
you're my mother too,
I will trust in you,
make me holy
like your holy Child.

Teaching Mary to Children

In my twenty-seven years of the Catholic Priesthood I've had many opportunities to give talks about Mary to adults and to children. The truths about Mary are the same for everyone; for adults they are received as information, for kids it's like they're taking photographs. It's said that kids think in pictures; they have incredible memories and to tell them a story or read to them could leave an imprint on their minds for life. Something to keep in mind is the fact that the simple, concrete examples used to explain the Faith to children work very well when explaining the Faith to people of other denominations. So having gone through these ideas directed to children, you can try them on your non-Catholic neighbors!

The Immaculate Conception

How to explain the Immaculate Conception to a child? The main point is to show that Mary was conceived without sin from the very first moment of her existence, because God had chosen her to be the mother

129

of his sinless Son. The question for the kids is something like this: If I came to your house for dinner and you were going to serve me delicious, steaming spaghetti – what kind of plate would you put it on, a clean one, or a dirty one? Their answer is always a clean one because nobody serves good spaghetti on a dirty plate! How about a cool drink of good spring water? What would happen to the good, clear water if the glass were grimy and hadn't been washed in months? It would become dirty and contaminated. So if kids would never put fresh clean water in a dirty glass, so God would never choose a dirty vessel when he desired to give us his pure and holy only-begotten Son. Just like the clean plate and the clear washed glass, he would make and use a pure, holy, clean vessel through which his spotless Son would come into the world - and that vessel is Mary, the Blessed Mother. God made her pure and immaculate from the first moment of her life in her mother's womb so she would be that pure vessel by which he would pour out his love, his only Son on the world.

The Immaculate Conception was like "Mary's baptism," or "vaccination" from Original Sin. At the moment she was conceived - from the very first instant of her existence - God preserved her from all stain of Original Sin. Now, some people outside the Church think that means that Mary was not saved; that Mary was not redeemed. Not true. Mary was redeemed most perfectly! There is the example of the fall into the "muddy stream": a person can be pulled out of it and cleaned up afterward or he can be caught before he hits the mud! Every human person (with the exception of Our Lady) has fallen into that muddy stream of Original Sin - it is the sad story of our fallen nature from the very beginning. Through Baptism we are "pulled out" and cleansed, through what Christ did on the cross for all mankind. *Mary was caught by God before she fell* - the merits of Christ were applied to her at the moment of her conception.

Mary, Mediatrix of Grace

In explaining this title of Mary to children, the idea is that when someone gives the source of something, they give the effects of that source as well. All graces come *from the Father, by the Son and in the Holy Spirit.* Christ, the Mediator between God and man, appointed Mary as the channel, the Mediatrix of all his graces. When the world received the *Source* of Grace, Jesus Christ, through Mary's "Yes", it also received *every grace* that comes from him. For example, if someone gave away a large piece of farm land which included a well and a small lake, that person also gave away all the water that would come from that well and any fish caught from the lake from that time on. So if Christ who is the Well of Living Water came to us through Mary, it is logical to say that all the other graces that come from Christ come through her as well.

Another example a child will understand is the father of the family who goes to work, earns the paycheck, and gives it to his wife who uses it for household needs and gives the kids their allowance. The husband earned the check, but does it take anything away from him if he wants to give the money to the wife for family use and to distribute to the children? The husband and wife are so closely united that the wife, making use of the money, does precisely what the husband would do. Mary, whose will is perfectly in accord with the will of Christ, distributes Grace to the world and to her spiritual children exactly as Christ would do.

Why Mary is Honored

Noah's Ark has caught the fascination and attention of children for countless generations, but the Old Testament tells of another "Ark" that gives a perfect example of why the Blessed Mother should be honored and revered. The Ark of the Covenant - a sort of Biblical preview of our present day tabernacle - is a symbol of the dignity and spiritual status held by Mary as Mother of God. Any child can probably tell us what was in Noah's Ark, and it would be a great blessing for kids to know the four sacred things in the Ark of the Covenant, (realizing, of course, that this Ark is not a boat!). It contained the things held sacred by the Jewish people: the Ten Commandments, scrolls of Sacred Scripture, some manna from the desert, and a piece of Aaron's rod. Parents can expand on the stories of these individual items, which can provide additional interest, in telling their children the story of the Ark of the Covenant. The Jewish people respected the Ark because of what was in it. They honored the Ark, but they didn't worship the Ark.

Now Mary, as the mother of Jesus, contained within her the Son of God, the Second Person of the Blessed Trinity, so she can be called an Ark as well. We respect and honor her as the Ark of the New Covenant because Mary held within herself something far greater than what the Ark of the Old Covenant contained. If the Jewish people respected and revered the Ark of the Covenant in the Old Testament for what was inside it, how much more should Mary, the New Ark of the Covenant, who held God himself within her, be honored and revered! And we can tell our Protestant friends that we, like the Jewish people of the Old Testament, revere our Ark, we don't worship our Ark!

In his talk called *Mary as the Ark of the Covenant,* Scott Hahn describes the visitation of Mary to Elizabeth, whose unborn son, John the Baptist, *leaped* for joy inside her womb at the sound of Mary's voice. That same word for *leaping* is used in the story of the Ark of the Covenant being brought into the presence of King David, where David *leaped* in joy before the Ark; a beautiful parallel showing Jesus living in Mary, the New Ark of the Covenant, to be greater than the holy relics within the Old Testament Ark of the Covenant.

Reverence for the Ark in the Old Testament is emphasized by the story of the servant who was struck dead when he put out his hand to touch it! That Ark was something very sacred and holy, as is Mary, the holy Ark of today. That's why it isn't wise to "mess with" the Blessed Mother! It is a warning to those who criticize the Mother of God, who downplay devotion to her, who deny the rightful place God has given to the New Ark of the Covenant. If that's the way God treated those who merely touched the Ark in the Old Testament, imagine the position of those who downgrade Mary today!

The New Eve

Children love Bible stories and the doctrine of the New Eve I have found young minds to grasp easily. When Christ is referred to as the Second Adam, as St. Paul does, they automatically think, "Who is the Second Eve?" Mary is the only one who fits the part. The first Adam and Eve were created without sin; since the New Covenant is greater than the Old Covenant, the new Adam and Eve must also be created without sin, so there is Jesus, God himself made man, and Mary, who is the Immaculate Conception. Kids are intrigued by the Old Testament story of the serpent - a fallen angel, Lucifer - and Adam and Eve. In the

136

New Testament they find a good angel, Gabriel, coming to the New Eve, Mary, who gives birth to the New Adam, Christ. In the Old Testament the serpent-angel offered Eve a temptation to evil; in the New Testament the good Angel offered Mary a proposition for grace. Eve sinned and said no to God, which brought us sin and death; Mary said yes to God and brought us grace and life.

The Holiness of Mary

How to get across to kids the sense and scope of Mary's holiness? One example from Scripture is the image of trees and the fruit they produce. Jesus says a good tree produces good fruit, a bad tree bad fruit. We say in the Hail Mary, "Blessed is the fruit of your womb, Jesus." Have the kids consider that when Jesus, who is the holy and all-perfect God, decided to become a little boy he chose Mary to be his mother. He made her to be the good and perfect tree since he would be the fruit that came from her. Have them think of the holiness of Christ, the source of goodness, the Second Person of the

137

Blessed Trinity eternally existing, of how holy he must have made that tree to have the fruit be Christ himself whose own words are, "A good tree produces good fruit."

We could ask the kids Bishop Sheen's question: If you had the power and the opportunity to pre-exist and create your own mother, how would you make her? What kind of mother would you make for yourself? Wouldn't she be the best, the holiest, the most beautiful, the most loving, the most gentle, the most tender, the most affectionate mother? No one but Jesus had that opportunity; only the Son of God could make His own Mother, and he did. He is the only one who ever pre-existed his mother.

A common example from creation is the relationship between the sun and the moon. Christ of course is the sun, the generator of light, and Mary is like the moon, having no light in and of herself. All her holiness is a gift from God, the pure and full reflection of Christ's holiness, just as the moon, which does not generate its own light but reflects the light of the sun. This holiness

138

of Mary, though a reflected holiness, is the holiness of Christ modified for our human sight. Just as human eyes cannot gaze directly at the sun, so the brilliance of the holiness of Christ is seen in the "full moon" of Mary for, like the moon, Mary was made for our night. There are many people weak or devoid of faith, or so steeped in sin by having rejected Christ that they seem to be living in endless night - but that moon still shines! A man I know had been away from the sacraments for twenty-five years but never failed to say a few Hail Marys, or a decade of the rosary before going to sleep. That grace was the moonlight of Mary shining in his darkness, for eventually he came back to Christ and the sacraments and attends daily Mass. Mary, the moon in his darkness, never stopped shining upon him the reflected light of her Son.

Should a thinking teen or young adult make the objection that Mary is praised too much, and that this takes away from the glory God alone deserves, it could be pointed out that God created her so holy that she deserves

139

the praise and honor the Church bestows on her. She can be presented as God's Masterpiece, his own great work of art! Objectors can be asked to imagine, upon visiting Michelangelo's studio, his reaction if they shrugged their shoulders and said of his Pieta: "There's nothing very special about that!" Imagine the artist's reaction if they ignored his work altogether! Would it take anything away from Michelangelo if they said, "What a magnificent work of art!" Would he take offense? Not at all. It is almost insulting to think that God is offended when Mary is praised. "Hail Mary, full of grace," is what he himself told the angel to say to her; that certainly doesn't take anything from him. As a matter of fact, it's a compliment. God could never be offended when praise, honor and glory are given to something he created, especially when it's Mary, his masterpiece!

Mary as Intercessor

With regard to Mary's intercessory power, kids love the story of the Wedding

Feast of Cana. "They have no more wine," Mary appealed to Jesus, and at her request, ordinary water became the best wine. He answered her petition with a miracle! So Mary is a proven intercessor. The story of Our Lady of Lourdes and Bernadette, and the many miracles that took place, is also attractive for kids. Instilling in their minds this intercessory power of Mary, their real spiritual mother, to answer all kinds of prayers will deepen their faith in the supernatural and imbed a lasting trait of confidence in God. I like to teach them this by way of a phrase: *I'll pray for you and you pray for me, and Mary, Jesus' mother will pray for us!*

St. Louis de Montfort in his book, *True Devotion to Mary*, uses the example of a child with an apple who wanted to make a gift to the king. The apple was bruised - nowhere near the status of a king's gift. So he went to the queen who took it to the kitchen, peeled away the bad spots, sliced it artistically and garnished it on a beautiful silver tray. What a proper gift for a king!

141

This is what Mary does for our prayers according to de Montfort.

The Offering

My Queen, take up my appled life
And place it firm beneath your knife,

And slice it open, cut in deep,
Dig out the worms that never sleep
And pare away my blemished skin –
What hidden rotting hides within –

Then blend into your recipe
Whatever good is left of me

So let your serving to the King
Be now my perfect offering!

There is also the example of a bridge. A bridge is a means of getting from one place to another. Mary was the "bridge" by which Jesus came to us. We can ignore or avoid the bridge if we choose, jumping into the water and swimming against the current to get to the other side - but the "bridge" will still be

there. It was God's intention for his Son
Jesus to come across from eternity to human
life by the "bridge" of Mary; and it is his
intention that she be the means by which we
go to Christ. Since he came to us through
Mary, should we not go through her to him?

Motherhood of Mary

Mary's Motherhood is something
that children intuitively embrace. When they
are told that by the sacraments they are one
with Christ, that Mary is the Mother of
Christ, and that that makes her their mother
too, they are given a permanent building
block of faith and the beginning of an interior
relationship with her. Mary is the mother of
Christ, who is the Son of God, and that Christ
is God, and that's why Mary is called the
Mother of God. She is also Mother of the
Church, of the Mystical Body of Christ. St.
Paul said the Church is the Body of Christ.
Now if Christ is the head of the Body, and we
are the members of the Body, isn't it logical
that Mary must not only be the mother of the
head but also the mother of the members,

Mother of Jesus and mother of us? A woman gives birth to a complete baby. Mary cannot be the mother of the head without being the mother of the complete Body of Christ. (Our friends in other church denominations will benefit from this logic!)

Sometimes people ask, "Did Mary have other children?" She had only one physical child - Jesus, but Mary has six billion spiritual children, and each of us is one of them! Scott Hahn talks about the Church as a family: We have God as our Father, we have Christ as our Savior and our Brother, we have the Angels and Saints as our relatives and cousins; and every family needs a mother. Emotionally, psychologically, spiritually we need a mother and that mother is Mary.

Mary and the Holy Spirit

The doctrine of Mary's relationship to the Holy Spirit includes symbols that always interest children. In the Bible there is the wind, the fire and the dove. They can get

144

some idea of his power by the great wind in the story of Pentecost, as well as of his inspiring wisdom in the flame of fire that settled on each disciple's head (without scorching their hair!). In other Gospel stories the loving presence of the Holy Spirit is manifested by the dove descending on Jesus in his baptism or the bright cloud at his Transfiguration. These symbols are necessary and can enrich faith, but the most complete image of the Holy Spirit is Our Lady herself.

If St. Paul can say that we are all temples of the Holy Spirit when in the state of grace, how much more so is Mary who is "full of grace" the Temple of the Holy Spirit! She is called Spouse of the Holy Spirit as well. But there is even a deeper understanding than this.

St. Maximilian Kolbe called her the most perfect *human image* of the Holy Spirit. He called her an *icon* of the Holy Spirit, a *mirror* of the Holy Spirit. The symbols of a tongue of fire or a great wind or dove are good images taken from the Bible, but are not quite adequate to help picture the reality of the Holy Spirit. Jesus said, "Who sees me sees the Father," since both are Persons; so the Holy Spirit, who is the third Person of the Blessed Trinity, is seen best when looking at Mary who could in effect say, "Who sees me sees the Holy Spirit." Of course, Mary isn't God - she is not a person of the Trinity, but because of her special union with the Holy Spirit she is the *physical representation* of the Holy Spirit. Looking at Mary's holiness, her purity, her virtues; knowing her tenderness, her comforting love for mankind, her Immaculate Heart, we see the Holy Spirit living within her in the most perfect way.

Mary Leading Us to Christ

In explaining to kids how Mary leads us to Christ, I refer to what Mary said in the Magnificat. My favorite translation has Mary saying, "My soul magnifies the Lord." Kids know what a magnifying glass is: it can make objects appear larger, and it can start a fire. And a common item in every child's life is eyeglasses. People don't complain about

146

glasses getting in the way of vision; no, glasses make seeing things larger and clearer. It's true that glasses come between the eyes and what is seen - but they don't get in the way. Now Mary didn't say, "My soul obscures the Lord, My soul obstructs the Lord." She said, "My soul *magnifies* the Lord," for she helps bring a larger and clearer presence of Christ into the lives of her children. Mary does not get in the way of our seeing Christ - she helps keep our sight directly on him, for her soul *magnifies* the Lord, just like the eyeglasses.

The magnifying glass is a reminder of Mary in another way. When it is held between the rays of the sun and is focused on paper or wood, it begins to burn. It is Mary's place to be between Christ, the sun, and the Christian soul, focusing his rays of grace upon it and setting it ablaze with love for God. Mary is not an obstruction between the soul and Jesus, she is absolutely necessary for the fire of love to grow!

I've also used when talking to children the image of the picture and the frame, Mary being like the frame and Christ like the picture. A good frame, well-designed and appropriate, draws attention to the painting rather than distracting from it. People wouldn't say, when viewing the Mona Lisa "What a beautiful frame!" Mary is the frame around Jesus, beautiful in herself but designed to enhance the picture and draw attention only to him. An idea for a little children's book would be: *Who Framed Christ?* Mary would be the answer, of course!

A discussion with the kids before or after Mass could include Mary as compared to the tabernacle. Mary was, and is, the living, breathing, walking tabernacle of Christ. We don't worship the tabernacle, we worship who's inside the tabernacle, Jesus, the Son of God in Holy Communion. The chalice and the monstrance can also be used in the same way. Mary is like a chalice which holds within it (just as she did those nine months long ago) the Body, Blood, Soul and Divinity of Our Lord Jesus Christ. And the beautiful monstrance in Benediction does not distract from the adoration of the Eucharist by the worshipers, but actually draws attention to Jesus Christ at its center. It is a major feature of devotion to Mary that she uses her beauty and her presence - like the monstrance - to focus attention on Christ.

Trusting in Mary

As for Mary being someone you can trust, I tell the kids about how God entrusted himself to Mary. I tell them how careful parents are to get a good babysitter! They don't go out searching the city streets inviting a stranger to babysit their child; they get the very best sitter they can. Wouldn't God do the same? Regarding his Son it wasn't just a weekend; it was nine months in Mary's womb and thirty years after that! And think of the adoption agencies that have to screen every family that wants a baby. A good deal of screening and discerning takes place before the right family is found. Would not God who is all wisdom have done the same? Wouldn't he have picked the very best couple to take care of his Son? Mary and Joseph

149

were the perfect ones, the only ones, for this special child.

The ultimate lifestyle is to follow Christ. It is the calling of every Christian to follow him, to imitate him, to be united with him. What was the first thing Jesus did when he took on our human nature? *He gave himself to Mary.* Where was the first place he chose to live? *Within Mary.* God was the first one to entrust himself to Mary; shouldn't we do the same? Shouldn't all children be taught to do the same? Jesus said, "Come, follow me; imitate me" (Mt 4:19). What better way to imitate Christ than to place ourselves in Mary's care and trust our children to the greatest mother there ever was? This trusting is the beginning of perfect imitation of Christ.

VIII.   St. Louis de Montfort and the Family

After Consecration

Mary is all of my life:
Moments show
As they go
She's their fountain
And their flow,
And when life's moment has passed
She'll hold another
To ever last –
Mary is all of my life.

Mary is all of my life:
Day by day,
Come what may,
She's my haven
And my way,
And when earth's pilgrimage ends
She'll be my beacon
As dark descends –
Mary is all of my life.

Mary is all of my life:

Year by year

She is here,

She's my world,

My atmosphere,

And when earth's living is done

We'll live forever

In Christ her Son –

Mary is all of my life!

St. Louis de Montfort and the Family

Before discussing St. Louis de Montfort's *True Devotion to Mary* as applied to the family, I think it is necessary to give a brief summary of his life and an outline of his spirituality, because St. Louis de Montfort is the saint God used to usher in the prophesied Marian Age which we now enjoy in the Catholic Church. There followed, after his appearance in Church History, a succession of great Marian Events: 1830 - the apparition of Our Lady and the Miraculous Medal, 1854 - the definition of the doctrine of the Immaculate Conception, 1858 - Our Lady's appearance at Lourdes; the visions in Knock in the late 1800s and in Fatima in 1917; there was also the establishment of various Marian movements and organizations such as the Legion of Mary, the Knights of the Immaculata and the Blue Army of Fatima; the defining of the doctrine of the Assumption of Our Lady and culminating in the reign of the great Marian pope, Saint John Paul II, whose motto was that of de Montfort himself: *Totus Tuus, I Am All Yours.*

His Life and Times

St. Louis de Montfort was born in Brittany, France on January 31, 1673, the second of eighteen brothers and sisters. It could be said that eleven of those children are saints today, since ten of them died in infancy after Baptism, leaving Louis to be the canonized one of that poor family. Of the eight siblings who lived to adulthood, three brothers became priests and the four sisters entered the convent. He was baptized the day after his birth and given the name Louis. The family name was Grignion. As a young man he took the name Marie for Confirmation.

While kneeling in prayer before a favorite image of the Blessed Mother in a Carmelite church in his town, he received his vocation, and at the age of twelve was studying in a Jesuit college in Rennes with 3,000 students. During this time in school he was already noted for having a great love for the Virgin Mary, a steady thirst for spiritual reading and a deep understanding of the spirit of poverty. At nineteen he entered the major seminary of Saint Sulpice in Paris, having walked 200 miles to get there! By the time he had reached Paris he looked very much the beggar and very little the seminarian, since, along the way, besides giving all his money to beggars, he exchanged his new and only suit for the ragged clothes of one of them!

Once accepted (reluctantly!) by the seminary, he became one of its brightest students and admitted that he read every book on the Blessed Virgin he could find. There were two ways by which he paid for his seminary training: by working as a librarian and by keeping vigil by the bodies of the deceased the night before a funeral, time he filled with prayer and spiritual reading.

At the time of his ordination in the year 1700, in addition to his appointment as chaplain to a hospital for the poor, Father de Montfort felt God was calling him to combat the rampant heresy of Jansenism, which denied the love and mercy of God. As an opponent of this heresy he preached missions and was attacked and persecuted by priests and bishops who had succumbed to the heresy. Although the Church was strong at this time, it was plagued by the difficulties caused by Jansenism and the effects of the Protestant revolt. Not being able to discern God's Will, he made a pilgrimage to Rome and sought a visit with the pope, Pope Clement XI. He had walked a thousand miles from Paris to Rome to ask, in meeting with the Holy Father, what he would have him do, and told Pope Clement of his desire to go to Canada as a foreign missionary. But the Holy Father, seeing the holiness and intelligence and courage of this priest, sent him back to France to be a missionary to his own people, to sanctify them by the practice of his priesthood and the preaching of Catholic Truth in his country threatened by Protestants and heretics.

In the remaining years of his priesthood he preached over 200 parish missions, and brought about many conversions. As he traveled - begging his food, his only possessions a Bible, rosary, notebook, and a small knife - he carved statues of the Blessed Virgin, composed verses of praise and wrote catechetical words to popular tunes of the day. One of his practices while giving a Mission was to have a book-burning in the town square of indecent, bad and anti-Catholic books brought by the people attending the Mission. This caused him much trouble from the Jansenist clergy, which he ignored but of which he never complained. When one bishop banned him from the diocese he willingly left and sought another. He preached love of the cross, devotion to Jesus and Mary and promoted the Confraternity of the Holy Rosary, as he was a Third Order Dominican.

During the short span of his sixteen years of priesthood, St. Louis de Montfort established three religious communities: the Company of Mary (known as the Montfort Fathers), the Daughters of Wisdom, and the Brothers of St. Gabriel. The first Daughter of Wisdom was Blessed Marie Louis Trichet, a woman who had been his sole nun for ten years before other sisters joined her!

St. Louis de Montfort had many attacks on his life. He was a tall, imposing figure and is known to have possessed great physical strength. On one occasion twelve men attacked him, but the would-be assassins got the worst of the fight! Two years before his death he was given a bowl of soup at one of the monasteries he visited; the soup was poisoned. He took only a taste but it was enough to ingest the deadly effects. He lived two more years and died at the age of 43, a priest for only 16 years. He was Beatified in 1888 and Canonized in 1947.

His Spirituality

St. Louis de Montfort wrote five major works as well as twenty-four thousand verses of poetry! His major works are: *The Secret of the Rosary, Friends of the Cross, The Secret of Mary, The Love of Eternal Wisdom, and the Treatise of the True Devotion to the Blessed Virgin Mary*, originally known as *The Preparation of the Reign of Jesus Christ*. The title *True*

Devotion to Mary is actually a nickname for the book.

St. Louis de Montfort predicted his spirituality would be accepted and practiced in the future and that it would be a powerful means of leading people to Jesus, so powerful, he said, that Satan himself would seek to keep it unknown, to impede its influence, and try to destroy it by attacking the *True Devotion* book itself. After his death in 1716, this book (his only manuscript) had not been published but had been hidden in a chest of old books for safe keeping during the time of "The Terror" and the French Revolution. For a hundred and twenty-six years the book that de Montfort predicted would be so powerful in converting souls and deepening the spiritual life of the Church through Mary lay like a treasure awaiting its time of discovery. And it was finally discovered - in vandalized condition: the first eighty pages had been ripped out! So Satan got his eighty pages, but the Church received the treasure of Christ-centered Marian devotion that has sanctified countless thousands of souls during these later centuries.

De Montfort spirituality is a Christ-centered spirituality, based on the place of the Blessed Mother in God's plan: How she was chosen by him to be the New Eve, chosen to be the living Ark of the Covenant, chosen to be the Mother of God. He explains her tri-fold role in Salvation History, showing how she is *Mother, Mediatrix,* and *Queen.* She is the *Mother of God,* by way of her part in the Incarnation of the Second Person of the Blessed Trinity, and the *Mother of all Humanity*, as her Jesus of Nazareth - the New Adam - expanded into all mankind and gave her to us at the foot of the Cross. She is the *Mediatrix* of Grace as shown in the Visitation, when she carried the unseen Christ to Elizabeth and sanctified John the Baptist in her womb; she is *Mediatrix* in the showing of the Christ Child to the shepherds and the Magi; she is seen as *Mediatrix* and Intercessor at the Wedding Feast of Cana; and as *Queen-Mother,* with Christ the King, she is *Queen of Heaven and Earth, Queen of the Universe* and, as de Montfort named her, *Queen of All Hearts*.

After showing Our Lady's important place in God's scheme of salvation, St. Louis goes on to show the need for union with her in order to be completely united to Christ. He proposes an Act of Total Consecration to Jesus - but *through Mary*. Just as Jesus came to us through Mary, was formed in her and raised by her, so, de Montfort says, that is the pattern for every Christian, the ideal for every soul: to be formed and raised by her into true identity with Christ. It is her ultimate mission. In the beginning, what did Christ do? He gave himself to Mary, made himself dependent upon her: for nine months in her womb, for the years of his infancy and youth, the time of his early manhood. It is de Montfort's spirituality that we do the same, through the Act of Total Consecration to Jesus through Mary. She has been called the "Mold of God"; de Montfort would call her the *Christ-mold* for mankind. By becoming totally dependent on her, as Jesus did, we are taken into the supreme and complete mystery

161

of our salvation and sanctification, where the Blessed Mother and the Redeemer are found in their proper place and relationship to us, and where the Holy Spirit pours his gifts and graces into us living in his perfect mold, Mary.

This Act of Total Consecration is prepared for by a thirty-three day preparation program in which de Montfort, through selected readings and prayers, lays the groundwork for the eventual giving of one's self to Jesus through Mary. The first twelve days are spent in trying to rid ourselves of the spirit of the world, followed by seven days growing in the knowledge of self; then there is a week of growing in knowledge of the Blessed Mother, climaxing with a week of growing in the knowledge of Christ. Then follows the choosing of a feast day of the Blessed Virgin when the formal act of consecration is made. We "pick a day and give ourselves away!" the old saying goes. A handwritten copy of the consecration is then made, and after Mass, after receiving Communion, we pray our consecration and give ourselves totally to Jesus through the Blessed Mother.

What we offer in the consecration is literally *everything:* All of our *material* possessions, all we own and all we are: home, car, furniture, bank account, our work, our retirement, our personal belongings, all our family and social connections - our life itself, past, present and future. We give all our *spiritual* goods - our prayers, our works, our joys, our sufferings (It's like a lifetime Morning Offering when we make this consecration to Jesus through Mary!). We give the value of all of our good actions, our merits, prayers, indulgences - everything is given to the Blessed Mother, Mediatrix of all Graces, for her to distribute as she determines.

This means that from the Consecration Day on, we try to live what is called "the holy slavery of love", where all we own belongs to the Blessed Mother. We have yielded all our freedoms and have become her possession. We trust her totally and try never to be uneasy with anything

163

past, present or future. As we live out this consecration, this holy slavery, Our Lady gives precious guidance in virtue and protection from sin and evil, and increases daily our ability to depend on her for everything, so that we do God's Will and become a living image and presence of Jesus Christ.

Marian Devotion and the Family

Devotion to Mary, and in particular St. Louis de Montfort's True Devotion, always brings special graces to a family. The following are ten recommendations for honoring our Blessed Mother and putting devotion to her into practice; I know from experience with many Catholic families that faith can be deepened, love safeguarded and peace assured in any home where devotion to the Mother of God is practiced.

1) *Consecrate your children to the Blessed Mother* and celebrate their baptismal days. At my sisters' and my own baptism our

164

parents consecrated us to the Blessed Mother. I would encourage you to consider this, for grandchildren as well. After a baptism ask the priest to say a special prayer of dedication or consecration of the child to the Blessed Mother.

I guarantee that if you do this she will always take care of those children. I also encourage celebration or at least recognition of a child's baptismal anniversary by giving a religious present on the day of their baptism each year, as a reminder of how important the day is.

St. Louis de Montfort thought so much of his baptism that he dropped his family name Grignion for Montfort, the city where he was baptized!

2)   *Make sure there is a statue or picture of the Blessed Mother in the home* - the more beautiful the better! It will be something of her that will be imbedded in the children's memories as they grow. A lighted candle or flowers on her feast days will enhance those memories.

St. Louis loved the Blessed Mother so much that, as mentioned above, he carved statues of her, and on his deathbed, along with a crucifix, held a little statue of the Blessed Mother.

3)	*Have a crucifix in the house* - perhaps in all the major rooms of the house. When we were little, my father gave each of us a personal crucifix, something special, made in France of rosewood and bronze. De Montfort loved the crucifix. He said we could learn more by long looks at the crucifix and meditating upon it than by reading any other book. His whole life was one of crosses, and to those who received his spiritual direction he would sometimes end his letters with the words "May God send you many crosses." He knew the value of suffering. His love for the crucifix at one point in his life drove him to inspire a whole city, and many nearby towns, to build a Calvary seventy feet high, which took over fifteen months to finish and was topped with a crucifix fifty feet in height that could be seen for miles around. (That Calvary had its own special "cross," for it was totally destroyed by the enemies of the Church days after the work was completed!)

Though a home may house a good Christian family, it is the crucifix - and the understanding of it - that makes a Catholic home.

4)   *Have the Sacred Heart enthroned in the home.* St. Louis de Montfort was utterly committed to establishing the "Reign of Christ" in the hearts and lives of all mankind; it is the reason he wrote the *True Devotion to Mary,* which is actually an expansion of the last four chapters of his book, *Love of Eternal Wisdom.* It is in this work that he makes known the four ways to obtain union with Christ in order to bring about the Reign of Jesus Christ in souls. The first way is *ardent desire:* there must be a conscious, deliberate desire to be one with Jesus; secondly, *constant prayer* to acquire this union with Christ; the third way is to *practice self discipline* and *mortification* and the fourth is to take on *the practice the True Devotion to the Blessed Mother.* The *True Devotion* volume outlines what it means to practice this devotion. By dedicating and consecrating the home to the Sacred Heart of Jesus, families

enter into this very Catholic way of holiness, fostering the Reign of Christ. The booklet of the *Enthronement of the Sacred Heart* is easily attainable at most religious stores or on the Internet, as is a picture of the Sacred Heart which is hung in the home at the culmination of the Enthronement service. I encourage all Catholic families to pick an appropriate day (the feast day of the Holy Family, Christ the King, the Sacred Heart or Corpus Christi) and let the Reign of Christ enter your home and your life.

5)   *Feature the rosary in the family.* If possible, say the family rosary every day. Practically everyone has heard Father Patrick Peyton's phrase, "The family that prays together stays   together." He affirmed that where the rosary is said there would be peace in that home and in that family. If the children are young and can't say the whole rosary, at least say one decade with them as a family. "A decade a day keeps the devil away!" is a motto to be passed on to the kids. (I often tell them of a T-shirt I once saw that had CALL YOUR MOTHER printed on the

front and SHE HASN'T HEARD FROM
YOU IN DECADES! on the back!) De
Montfort was a great promoter of the rosary,
which he included in every Mission he
preached. The rosary was one of the four
personal items of property he possessed at
death.

6)   *Have a great love for the
sacramentals of the Church*. St. Louis says
that every Catholic should wear something
Catholic, whether it be the brown scapular or
a religious badge of the Sacred Heart,
crucifix pin, etc. I'm sure if the miraculous
medal had been available in his lifetime (it
was given in 1830, about a hundred years
after his death) he would have promoted it
with zeal! Today many options are available
for Catholics to quietly profess their Catholic
Faith: patron saint medals, crosses and
crucifixes on chains, holy cards and prayer
leaflets that can be politely given to others,
etc. Kids love receiving and wearing
sacramentals; parents and grandparents
should have a real interest in equipping each
member of the family with their own

personal sacramentals, some of which will be with them for years, helping to keep them close to the Faith. In explaining the True Devotion to the Blessed Virgin St. Louis recommended wearing a blessed chain, worn either around the neck or on the wrist as a bracelet; my Mom and Dad had rings made of chain to remind them of their total gift of self to Mary. Another favorite sacramental of de Montfort's was the brown scapular and, in keeping with his devotion to the Mother of God, I recommend to all the wearing of and enrollment in two of my favorites: the brown scapular and the miraculous medal.

7)   *Read the True Devotion to Mary and make it your own.* The spirituality of St. Louis de Montfort has influenced some of the most important theologians, saints and holy people of recent centuries. The Spiritual Childhood and the theme of Total Trust, expounded by St. Therese, the Little Flower, is a basic de Montfort theme that was being promoted in the last part of the 19th century when St. Therese would have been aware of and influenced by it.

170

St. Maximilian Kolbe is another saint who absorbed the spirituality of St. Louis, as well as Saint John Paul II, who said that he had read and re-read the de Montfort writings and took the saint's spiritual motto as his own papal one, *Totus Tuus*. Many of the popes in the last century – Pope Pius IX, St.Pius X, Leo XIII, Benedict XV, Pius XI, and Pius XII – all read, studied, and lived the spirituality of the True Devotion to Mary. Blessed Mother Teresa lived it heroically; Venerable Matt Talbot, an alcoholic in Ireland was converted through reading it; Servant of God Frank Duff, founded the Legion of Mary on it.

8)   *Make and live the Total Consecration according to St. Louis de Montfort.* This means trying to imitate the virtues of our Blessed Mother, trying to live the consecration within your family in your Catholic home. It means trying to *be* Mary, to live as she would in your circumstances. It means watching TV as the Blessed Mother would; using only the language that the Blessed Mother would use; making sure

you're doing whatever the Blessed Mother would want you to do. You have probably seen the WWJD bracelets: *What Would Jesus Do?* After the consecration is made we are called to wear the spiritual WWMD bracelet: *What Would Mary Do?* (What Would *Montfort* Do?) If we could always do what Mary, who was the First Christian, would do, then obviously we would be doing what Christ would do, and that is the essence of Christian behavior.

9)   *Read a complete life of St. Louis de Montfort;* get to know the saint of True Devotion and his Marian way. One recommendation is *Wisdom's Fool* by Eddie Doherty, available from Montfort Publications, Bay Shore NY, official publisher of all Montfort publications. For children there is *St. Louis de Montfort* by Mary Fabyan Wyndeatt, published by TAN. I cannot emphasize enough how important and beneficial this de Montfort connection is to the Catholic family: it will prevent the family from spiritual stagnation in a pagan society; it will influence the family and its

members to be more than average in their faith, and will raise them to the *normal* status of genuine Catholic family life in which saints are formed.

10) *Try to become active in an organization that promotes this total consecration to Jesus through Mary*; for example, The Knights of the Immaculata, The Blue Army, The Legion of Mary. These organizations know and apply the de Montfort principles and spirituality, and since I am personally experienced with the Legion of Mary I recommend it to you. My parents met in the Legion, which became their expression of the Catholic vocation. Their honeymoon was comprised of a visit to Lourdes where they consecrated their marriage to the Blessed Mother, followed by four weeks in Dublin where they spent many hours with the founder, Frank Duff, living and learning the Legion first hand. I joined the Legion of Mary along with my two sisters when I was ten years old and have continued in it ever since, up to and including my priesthood. I have often mentioned the Legion in my talks

173

on Parenting, since it is something both parents and kids can belong to. By its twofold membership of active apostleship and personal prayer the whole family can be involved. At one time I had eight groups of the Legion in my parish: two for children, one especially for "Moms" and the others for mixed family-styled groups of men and women, single, married, retired. There are several reasons I could give to encourage you to look into of the Legion of Mary, but the most important is its connection to St. Louis de Montfort. It was out of a discussion on True Devotion to Mary that the Legion of Mary came into being; St. Louis is called "The Tutor" of the Legion and its prophet. Here is a quote from his writings:

"I clearly foresee that raging beasts will come in fury to tear to pieces with their diabolical teeth this little book and him whom the Holy Ghost has used to write it, or at least to bury it in the darkness and silence of a coffer, that it might not appear. . . This vision encourages me and makes me hope for

174

great success, that is to say, for a mighty legion of brave and valiant soldiers of Jesus and Mary, of both sexes, to fight the devil, the world, and corrupt nature in those more than ever perilous times that is to come!"

We have seen how these words were fulfilled regarding the *True Devotion* book buried in darkness for over a hundred years and discovered in damaged condition. I believe the second part of this prophecy has also been fulfilled: Since 1921 there has been a "legion" of "brave and valiant" souls who fight the evil of sin in their own lives and in the lives of others, its main motive: *holiness,* in themselves and in others. Should this not be the ultimate purpose and goal of every Catholic family, especially in these particular "perilous times" in which we live? May "Our Lady of the True Devotion" bless and prosper all Catholic families through the charism, mission and patronage of St. Louis Marie de Montfort!

IX. Enthronement of the Sacred Heart in the Home

Jesus of the Sacred Heart

O Jesus of the Sacred Heart,
Come and live in me:
Come fill this body,
This life, with Your Grace –
Turn then Your Face
toward others.

O Jesus of the Sacred Heart,
Come and give through me:
Take these two hands
That are able to bear –
Teach them to share
with others.

O Jesus of the Sacred Heart,
Come and love in me:
Here is a heart
That is beating for You –
Pour Your Love through
for others!

Enthronement of the Sacred Heart in the Home

It is appropriate in an explanation of devotion to the Sacred Heart in the Church that there be direct allusion to the Blessed Sacrament. Father John Hardon, S.J. said there can never be a separation between devotion to Christ in the Eucharist and devotion to his Sacred Heart. It was during exposition of the Blessed Sacrament that Our Lord appeared to St. Margaret Mary and revealed his desire for devotion to his Sacred Heart. Since in Holy Communion Christ is present in his entirety - Body, Blood, Soul and Divinity - adoration to the Sacred Heart of Jesus, present in the Eucharist, is the soul of Eucharistic spirituality.

What Holy Scripture Says

On one occasion only does the Bible mention Christ's request to imitate himself, referring to his own personal qualities: *"Learn from me, for I am meek and humble of heart" (Mt 11:29).*

The verses about Calvary include the thrust of the soldier's lance into the lifeless side of Christ. Eyewitnesses attest to the piercing of his Heart, because blood and water issued forth, certifying his death and manifesting the thought of many spiritual writers that this was the moment of the *conception* of the Church, just as the wind and tongues of fire were to acclaim the *birthday* of the Church at Pentecost. The water symbolized the sacrament of Baptism that washes away sin, and the accompanying blood represented the Holy Eucharist. This doctrinal foundation of devotion to the Sacred Heart of Jesus from Sacred Scripture - Our Lord's own words and the piercing of his Heart on Calvary - meant that the graces of his Redemption were now being poured out upon the world.

A Little Bit of History

At the moment of the Incarnation, when God became man, the Sacred Heart of Jesus - formed in the womb of Mary, directly below her own Immaculate Heart - beat for

178

the first time and he began his incarnate life on earth.

There is a reference at the Last Supper, where St. John, the "Beloved Disciple", leaned upon the Heart of Christ. (St. John has been called the "Apostle of the Sacred Heart", as well as Mary's own priest and apostle.)

Devotion to the Sacred Heart is actually very ancient. Many of the early Church Fathers referred to the Heart of Christ in their writings. But there was a time in Church history when devotion to the Sacred Heart was more prominent, and that was because it was being attacked by the followers of Jansenism - one of the most serious heresies ever to afflict the Church. Jansenism taught that Christ did not die for all, but only for a certain number of people or for certain predestined souls; it taught that not everyone received the grace of salvation, and it denied the doctrine of free will. But this heresy was especially serious because it denied the love of God and the mercy of God.

179

St. Francis de Sales, one of the great opponents of Jansenism, was the founder of the Visitation Order, and his books, *Introduction to the Devout Life* and *Treatise on the Love of God* - still available today - were very influential in opposing Jansenism. Along with St. Margaret Mary and St. Claude de la Colombiere, they spread the Love of God and the Mercy of God, through devotion to the Sacred Heart of Jesus, and completely destroyed the Jansenist heresy. Jesus manifested his Sacred Heart as a symbol of God's unconditional love for each member of the human race, but reminded them of their indifference when to St. Margaret Mary he said, *"Behold the Heart which so loves mankind and receives so little love in return."*

Through the years 1673 to 1675, at the Visitation Convent in Paray-le-Monial in France, St. Margaret Mary Alacoque, a young religious sister, considered to be the most unassuming and simple of all the nuns in the convent, received apparitions from Christ himself presenting his appeal for

180

devotion to his Sacred Heart. Our Lord chose this humble, cloistered, contemplative Visitation nun, whose life had been filled with many crosses, to be an apostle of the Sacred Heart to the Pope, the Church, and ultimately the whole world.

As it became known that she was receiving apparitions, she was made fun of, ridiculed and called a fraud by the other sisters. It was only when St. Claude de la Colombiere became her spiritual director that she began to experience some consolation and was able to more freely spread this message throughout the Visitation Order. Eventually it became a part of the Jesuit spirituality and finally influenced the entire Church.

Devotion to the Sacred Heart of Jesus should not be considered an isolated, private or personal devotion of a few people - it is a devotion at the heart of Catholic theology and belief.

From Father Hardon we have six highlights underlying doctrines of the Faith that support this central devotion:

Underlying Doctrines

1)   *God created the human race out of
love.* Since God was perfectly happy in and
of himself it was not for himself that he
created mankind and the angels, but to share
his overflowing love with all creation,
intending every angel and every human being
to live with him for all eternity.

2)   *The Incarnation actually happened;* it
was out of love for a sinful human race and a
desire to redeem it that God became man, to
save all from the penalty of sin.

3)   *God assumed a human will that he
might freely choose suffering and death.*
Since God cannot suffer, it was decreed for
the second person of the Blessed Trinity live
in a human nature so that he could suffer and
die. In the second person in the Blessed
Trinity there beats the Sacred human Heart of
Jesus.

4)   *The Church teaches that Jesus died
for all mankind.* God gives everyone enough
grace to be saved. If a person is not saved, it

is not God's fault. It is the person's own free will that has rejected his love and mercy.

5)   *God has given each human being a free will* with the freedom to choose to love him and deny self or reject him and love self.

6)   *Every human being is called to respond to God's love*, which Jesus showed by dying on the cross and by giving us his Heart. In one apparition of emanating light - symbolizing Jesus as the Light of the World - he showed St. Margaret Mary his Sacred Heart roped and crushed with thorns, with the wound of the spear, bleeding for our salvation.

So all are exhorted to love God with a *heart for Heart* devotion, professing to believe that he loves the human race, that he became man to die for sin, that he gives every soul enough grace to be saved, and that his Sacred Heart waits with all love and mercy for the selfless response of love from all mankind.

The Twelve Promises

183

St. Margaret Mary received numerous promises from Jesus in the apparitions, which are found in her letters. They have been simplified and distilled into twelve, and are very important to share with fellow Catholics because they embody the reasons why the Sacred Heart should be enthroned in homes, and list the many blessings and benefits received when the Enthronement takes place.

1)　　Jesus promises that those devoted to his Sacred Heart *will receive all the graces necessary for their state in life.* Sincere and loving devotion to his Sacred Heart assures each follower of the presence of all the graces necessary to endure, develop and fulfill their obligations, demands, aspirations and desires of their chosen lifestyle. This is documented in St. Paul, when Jesus said, "My grace is sufficient for you."

2)　　*"I will establish peace in your family."* This is the most rewarding and should be the main reason for a Catholic family to enthrone the Sacred Heart of Jesus in the home, in the light of the unrest and disturbance in present-day society, which can slip so easily into the shelter of a home. When the consecration is made in the proper spirit and as the family strives to live the consecration daily, the peace of Christ descends on the family and each member benefits from this special gift, as he promised in the Bible: "Peace I leave with you, my peace I give you."

3)　　*"I will bless every place in which the picture of my Heart is exposed and honored."* This could be in a home or a place of business, a nursing home or even a classroom. Many people belonging to the Sacred Heart Auto League have a picture of the Sacred Heart on the dashboard as a reminder of the promise of Jesus to bless the place where his picture is displayed. (Unlike St. Christopher, who, some people claim, will get out of a car going over the speed limit, the blessing of the Sacred Heart is permanent!)

　　　　I used to know a real estate agent who carried a picture of the Sacred Heart of Jesus in his briefcase; his business did very well, but since then it seems the St. Joseph statue has taken over that blessing! The point to consider is that the exposure of the picture on a wall or in a car is not sufficient to merit the blessing promised; it must be honored. How is the image of the Sacred Heart of Jesus honored? By respect and reverence. Some families make it the centerpiece of a small shrine, perhaps on a mantle, where flowers and a candle could be set. Walking by that "shrine", or noticing it from a distance in the room, can be an occasion of grace, a reminder of spiritual things in busy or hectic moments of family life. It can inspire a short prayer like "Most Sacred Heart of Jesus, have mercy on me," "Sacred Heart of Jesus, I place my trust in you," or "Jesus, I believe in your love for me." Many families I know make it the focus of family prayer time.

4)   *"I will console you in all your difficulties."* Notice he does not say, "I will take away all your difficulties," but "I will console you in all your difficulties." Jesus does not promise that the family will be exempt from problems or crises; he calls

attention to his permissive Will which allows all things to happen but gives, in his loving providence, protection and care, strength and comfort in the midst of suffering and trials.

5)   *"I will be your refuge during life, and especially at the hour of your death."* The hour of death is the time when God's grace is needed most. Fr. Faber reminds us that evil spirits tend to be present around a deathbed, because it is the last chance to induce the soul to despair and to turn from God's mercy. Devotion to the Sacred Heart of Jesus will supply all the graces necessary to endure the trials of this life and to pass peacefully through the door of death to life to come.

6)   *"I will shed abundant blessings upon all your undertakings."* Work, parenting, marriage, personal interests, daily activities, long-range plans, all of life will be included in his care.

7)   *"Sinners will find in my Heart a fountain and boundless ocean of mercy."* Those who have been away from the Church and the sacraments for great lengths of time, or those who have done things they consider

unforgivable by God, should have recourse to the Sacred Heart of Jesus, for looking into his Heart they will find not a limited fountain but a *limitless ocean* of Mercy. They should realize that what the sea is to floating boats, his Heart of infinite mercy and love is to the sinner who comes back to him. St. Margaret Mary said that sins in relation to the mercy of God are like drops of water sprinkled into a fiery furnace.

8)   *"Tepid souls shall become fervent."* Tepid, of course, means lukewarm. Turning to Christ's Heart, lukewarm souls will become more fervent and devout. The sad condition of faith and devotion in the Church today is that "Weekend Catholics" and the "Christmas and Easter" Catholics are not hard to find. Catholic Life, which should be a burning joy, has simmered to lukewarm acceptance and joyless affiliation in many places. Devotion to the Sacred Heart can be the means of inspiring the lukewarm Catholic to be inflamed with the dynamic *life* of Grace by which personal faith and loving service prosper.

9)   *"Fervent souls will rise speedily to great perfection."* Fortunately, the Church has many fervent members, priests, nuns and laity who give their lives in special sanctifying ways to the Church. But much more is needed. Saint John Paul II appealed for *saints*, heroic lovers of God who will respond to the longing call of the Sacred Heart of Jesus: love for Love! This is his promise to the fervent souls of the Church, that he offers them the prospect of spiritual fulfillment, the assurance of genuine sanctity.

10)   *"I will give to priests the power to touch the most hardened hearts."* Being a priest, this naturally is my favorite promise. I have seen its effects many times in my priestly work and there are countless stories of people being converted through devotion to the Sacred Heart. One of my stories occurred when I was deacon assigned to a parish. There was a very sick man in the nursing home visited by the parish priests. He would never talk to them and refused the invitation to pray. He had totally rejected God. Oftentimes, when the priest in charge

of the parish Legion of Mary assigned the members to try to visit the man, he would actually yell at them to get out of his room. Being conscious of this particular Promise, the Legion members decided to make a novena to the Sacred Heart for his conversion. With the completion of the novena they attempted to try him again. This time he was open to their visit and accepted a crucifix, kissing it several times; he agreed to a visit by the priest and died shortly after receiving the sacraments. It is an example of the power of the Sacred Heart, shown through souls who believe in his Promises and act on them.

11)   *"Those who spread this devotion will have their names written on my Heart, never to be erased."* This promise to those who spread devotion to the Sacred Heart should hold great consolation for them, and should be an inducement to others to begin promoting it in earnest. Considering who it is who said these words, the intimacy they offer, and the honor of having their name "written in gold on the Heart of Jesus Christ,"

190

as St. Margaret Mary said, the choice to promote this devotion should be a foregone decision - especially when there are people who commit to picking up trash along a highway just to have their name on an "Adopt a Highway" sign or who donate huge sums of money to be listed on some prestigious roster of Benefactors or bronze memorial plaque! I once mentioned in a homily the idea of getting a box of Sacred Heart holy cards to enclose in letters and greeting cards. A week later I got a call from the local religious store asking that I stop sending people for Sacred Heart holy cards until they could replenish their stock! It's a small thing to do to have your name written forever on the Heart of Christ!

12)   I think this is perhaps the greatest of all the Promises. *"I promise you that in the excessive mercy of my Heart, my all powerful love will grant to those who receive communion on the First Friday of the month for nine consecutive months the grace of final repentance. They will not die in my displeasure, nor without the sacraments. My*

divine Heart will be their safe refuge at the last moment." This is the well known First Friday devotion consisting of mass on the First Friday of nine consecutive months, receiving holy communion in reparation for the sins committed against the Sacred Heart, and going to confession within eight days before or after the First Friday. The nine consecutive Fridays could be considered a novena. Think of it! The making of that novena of masses out of love for Jesus promises something unfathomable: to die with the sacraments and most likely with a priest. For the soul in the state of grace Jesus promises his comforting presence at life's last moment. For souls not in the state of grace Jesus will make sure a priest will be there for confession, communion and the final anointing. He says you will not die in my displeasure, which means dying in unrepentant mortal sin - in other words the grace of a deathbed conversion. It's a "Win-Win" situation: all these Promises guaranteed, for the grace and privilege of living a sincere and faithful devotion to the Sacred Heart of Jesus.

The Enthronement Ceremony

Why Enthronement of the Sacred Heart of Jesus? In the Our Father we pray, "Thy kingdom come." How is this kingdom of God established on earth? Through the reign of Jesus Christ: by his Eucharistic reign in the Blessed Sacrament, and by the reign of the Sacred Heart in the home. The family has been called the "domestic church", and the Enthronement ceremony is the liturgy of the domestic church as it brings about the reign of Christ in families now and ultimately in society. When a family makes the Enthronement, they are saying that Jesus Christ is King, Ruler and Lord of this family, as in the words of Joshua in the Old Testament: "As for me and my house, we will serve the Lord."

The first step in the Enthronement is to provide a quality picture or statue of the Sacred Heart of Jesus, large enough to have a prominent presence. (The Divine Mercy picture, as beautiful as it is, would not qualify because it does not show the Sacred Heart with the circling crown of thorns and the pierced wound in our Lord's side.) The next step is to decide on an appropriate place to display it, perhaps the main entranceway to the house or in a room where the family gathers most often. It should be highlighted in some way, such as with flowers, candles or some special light.

This Enthronement is intended to be the beginning of a new life for the family, and means the acknowledging of the authority of Jesus as King over that life. They should know that the word *enthronement* means to establish a throne or sacred place, as when Charlemagne was enthroned in the great Cathedral as Holy Roman Emperor. The importance of the name Sacred Heart should also be understood, because in Scripture the heart stands for *the whole person*. In the Bible the words, "Son, give me your heart" means "give me your whole self, will, intellect, memory, emotions." We hear too of people being warm hearted, softhearted, coldhearted,

194

or hardhearted. As for the word Sacred, it means being set aside for a holy purpose. The "Sacred Heart" is holy because it is the Heart of Jesus himself, who is the source of all holiness.

Since families are invited to establish Jesus as King and friend of their home, the ceremony should afford the opportunity for spiritual enlightenment and personal conversion for family members; therefore, it should not be a rushed ceremony. It should be something they study and prepare for. The ceremony is intended to be the beginning of a new spirituality, a concentrated living of their love for Jesus Christ as he wants to be known in the image of the Sacred Heart.

It is suggested that three days before the ceremony the family say the available Triduum prayers, a beautiful preparation for the Enthronement. It would enhance the event if they could go to Mass and Holy Communion for the three days beforehand, with confession, if needed, and try to attend Mass on the actual day. A Sunday afternoon has been found to be an ideal time,   but any special day could be chosen, such as an anniversary date or feast day if not planned for a Sunday, with every member of the family present, if possible.

Although it adds a special blessing to the event when a priest or deacon is present, it isn't actually necessary since the family does the consecrating, as in a marriage where the husband and wife do the marrying with the officiating priest as witness. Of course, it would add a certain "official" sense to the ceremony if the priest were present to give a short homily and a blessing at the conclusion of the event. Many people have never heard of this devotion, so it's a good idea to invite friends, neighbors and relatives. It is an indirect way to evangelize, and by inviting others they already become apostles of the Sacred Heart! After the ceremony a celebration with refreshments or a meal should be held in thanksgiving to God for this special grace.

The place of honor designated for the picture or statue should be separate from where the ceremony begins, providing the opportunity for a short procession. The priest, family, and guests gather in a separate room where the picture or statue and family Bible have been set aside. The blessing of the images could be done here if not done ahead of time. The father, or family member presiding, would carry the image of the Sacred Heart of Jesus and the mother an optional image of the Immaculate Heart of Mary - families often include both images. One or more of the children could carry a candle, flowers, or the family Bible with all processing to the main room where the Enthronement takes place. The idea of the procession is a reminder of the whole Church in procession on pilgrimage towards Heaven.

The Apostle's Creed is said by the family as an act of faith and reparation, and readings from the Bible follow. There are four that are most appropriate:

1)   *The Annunciation Narrative* of the Angel Gabriel, telling Our Lady of her maternity as   Mother of God and how she receives Jesus into her life, a

197

reference to the family receiving the Sacred Heart into their home (Lk 1:26).

2)   The story of *Zacchaeus*, the tax collector, to whom Jesus says, "Today I will abide in your home" (Lk 19:5).

3)   *The Road To Emmaus*, when the disciples say, "Lord, stay with us" (Lk 24:29).

4)   *Martha and Mary at Bethany,* where Jesus visits the home of his beloved friends. As Jesus had an intimate and spiritual relationship with Lazarus, Martha, and Mary, so the enthroned home is called to be another Bethany, a place where a special, increasingly intimate relationship is intended to develop between Jesus and all the members of the family (Jn 11:1).

The priest or deacon might give a homily here, or some other qualified person say a few words. With everyone kneeling around the image of the Sacred Heart (and the Immaculate Heart if included) the Act of Consecration is read, followed by recitation of the Our Father, Hail Mary, and Glory Be for both living and deceased members of the family, and those who were not able to be present. The Prayers of the Faithful are next, read by the priest, the father, or divided up among family members. The official dated certificate is then presented to the family, which is signed by all family members and by the priest, deacon or other Church representative as a witness. It is asked that the family frame the certificate and have it near the place of honor. This completes the ceremony.

It is recommended that the Act of Consecration be renewed annually, with the procession and renewal prayers optional. A simpler ceremony than the one described could be conducted and would be a valid enthronement, the main emphasis being the image (or images) in a prominent place and reverence for it by the family.

To make the ceremony a richer and lasting experience, the following suggestions may be considered. The family could add the practice of saying the well known Morning Offering, whereby they offer their prayers, works, joys and sufferings of the day for the intentions of the Sacred Heart.

Another way of practicing the devotion is to say a short prayer whenever the image of the Sacred Heart is seen or passed by during the day; or the family could gather there for family prayer. "Where two or more are gathered," Jesus said, "there I am in their midst" (Mt 18:20).

Other suggestions would be the making of the nine First Fridays, attending Mass on the feast day of the Sacred Heart every year, an occasional recitation of the Litany of the Sacred Heart - all are ways in which members of the newly enthroned family can truly deepen their love and respect for the Sacred Heart of Jesus.

In the evolving of this devotion to the Sacred Heart, it has become appropriate to include the Immaculate Heart of Mary in the enthronement ceremony. Where Jesus reigns as king, Mary reigns as queen. A companion picture or statue of Our Lady would complete the shrine honoring her Son and will add that mother's care to the times of stress and concern that arise in daily living.

The enthroned family is the domestic Catholic Church, praying for their personal and family intentions, of course, but for wider intentions also, such as protection from the encroaching evil in society, for the grace not to compromise with the widespread spirit of secularism and for the welfare of the universal Church suffering persecution and demonic attack. Having given to Jesus their "whole heart" and having accepted him as King and Mary as Queen of their home and lives, the enthroned family asks for the grace to welcome the Will of God and to worship his wisdom when suffering, trial, illness and death inevitably cast their shadow over their consecrated family life.

Complete information on the Enthronement of the Sacred Heart in the Home is available on the internet with a search to *Enthronement of the Sacred Heart.*

X.   The Family Rosary

The Woman of the Rosary

A Virgin sang in the summertime:

Soft was her song,

Soft as the rustle of grain,

Rich with the promise of Grain.

A Bride once sang in an autumn:

Happy her song,

Free as a leaf in the wind,

Sure as an oak in the wind.

A Mother sang in the wintertime:

Tender her song,

Sweet with the feel of a Child,

Warm with a love for her Child.

A Widow sang in the springtime:

Somber her song,

Sad as a hillside of stone,

Sad as a grave sealed in stone . . .

A Woman sings through the seasons —

Sings of the Grain,

Sings on the wind,

Sings in the stone,
Sings of her Child!
She sings of a Son who has grown –
A Son and a rolled-away stone!

The Family Rosary

"The Family That Prays Together Stays Together" - the slogan of Father Patrick Peyton's rosary crusade - if not as popularized as when he was alive promoting the family rosary, is still a true statement for every individual Catholic and in every Catholic Family. Today, when family life is fast eroding in the waves of modernism, secularism and socialism, it is crucial for the appeals made by Our Lady of Fatima for the saying of the daily rosary be heeded and acted upon by all Catholics, especially by the Catholic Family. The most effective and most powerful thing a person can do is pray. I believe the one important reason why the rosary is not more widely appreciated and prayed by more Catholics today is that they are not aware of the power of the rosary and the respect they should have for it. People are impressed by strength and power, by the promise, for example, of new medicines and drugs that can cure every illness! So here are some true stories of the power of the rosary that should be read and shared, so that the many graces promised by Our Lady will rain down on the Church, on the family, on our Nation and on the world.

One Rosary Was Enough!

Just one rosary made a difference. In the year 1840, a nineteen-year-old university student was having a crisis of faith. He couldn't be sure he believed in the Catholic religion. One day, as he wandered aimlessly through the streets of Paris, distressed by his spiritual trial, he strolled into the back of a Catholic church. A man was saying his rosary; he was devout and reverent and oblivious of his observer, who was the only other person in the church. At the sight of this man with a rosary in his hand, his doubt completely vanished and his faith was reaffirmed. The man praying the rosary was Dr. Andre Ampere of the University of Paris; we know him as the famous Catholic scientist and inventor, whose name has given our vocabulary technical words like amp and amplifier. The young man who had his faith strengthened that providential night was Frederick Ozanam, who in the following year founded the St. Vincent de Paul Society, which is now in every diocese in every country of the world. Later in 1921, in a branch of the St. Vincent de Paul Society, there appeared Frank Duff who founded the Legion of Mary. That one man praying in the darkened Parisian church never realized that his one rosary would affect the lives of millions, even down to our day.

The Traveling Rosary

When she appeared on February 11, 1858, to Bernadette at Lourdes, the Blessed Virgin Mary had the rosary over her right elbow. In the vision of Fatima on May 13, 1917 the rosary was held in her hand. From November 29 to January 3, 1932-1933, the Blessed Mother appeared thirty-three times in Beauraing, Belgium to five children and this time the rosary had moved from her hand to her fingertips. Without a doubt, the Blessed Mother wanted the rosary said. She spoke to the Fatima children and she said, "Pray the rosary every day; continue to pray the rosary; I want you to pray the rosary." Our Lady called herself the Lady of the Rosary. Out of all her 1,600 titles, she could have chosen her most exalted title - the Mother of God - or she could have chosen her second most exalted title, the Immaculate Conception, but no, she chose the Lady of the Rosary. From 1858 to 1917 to 1933, every time Our Lady has appeared she has asked by her actions and her words that the rosary be said. Twenty-eight out of thirty-three times that Our Lady appeared to the Belgian children; they dropped to their knees on the hard gravel, went into ecstasy and began praying the rosary. As they prayed the rosary, doctors attempted to verify the authenticity of the children's condition. They were stuck with pins, but didn't flinch or bleed. Cigarette lighters were lit underneath their hands but it did them no harm. Three strong men were unable to lift one seventy-pound girl. They were wrapped in ecstasy saying the rosary. Each night when the children had finished saying the rosary, church officials and theologians would question them. They were astounded by the answer to the question, "Why did you suddenly fall down and begin to pray the rosary?" "We had no choice," they said. "The Blessed Mother forced us to say the rosary!" That's how much she wants the rosary said.

Caught "Rosary-handed"!

In the year 1821 a train was going from Dijon to Paris carrying an elderly passenger. Sitting across from him was a young university student with a stack of textbooks. Presently, the old man got out his rosary and began to thumb the beads. The young student noticed, grinned and said, "You don't still believe in that silly superstition, do you?" The old man replied, "Yes, but you don't?" The young man commented that he did at one time, until he became educated at the university to the scientific age. The train began to slow down

208

and the elderly man prepared to rise. "Do you know how to read?" asked the student. "Yes", said the old man. "Let me send you a book", the young man said, "I think it will convince you of the enlightened position regarding the old superstitions." The old man nodded and from his pocket handed the young man his business card: Dr. Louis Pasteur, Department of Research, University of Paris. One of the most brilliant scientists of his day was caught praying his rosary on his way to work! It's fairly certain the young man never fulfilled his offer to send him a book! (Dr. Louis Pasteur, of course, became famous for his process of milk purification. I often joke with the kids in my parish, "When you go home, open the refrigerator, take out the milk and look for the word *pasteurized;* it means you'll be drinking genuine 'Catholic' milk!")

A Friend in Beads

His name is Bartolo Longo. He was born in 1841 in Naples and attended the University of Naples where he abandoned his

Catholic Faith. He got involved in the occult, and was eventually ordained a high priest in the Church of Satan. One of his friends had prayed a daily rosary for him from the time he left the Catholic Faith and eventually was able to convince Bartolo that he should abandon the Satanic church and start saying the rosary. With the praying of the rosary he was able to resist and break the hold the occult influence had on him. But although Bartolo separated from the satanic movement, he was convinced he could never be saved since he had been ordained a priest of the devil, and that there was a place waiting for him in hell. He believed there was no way God could ever have mercy on him. On October 9, 1872, in one of his deepest moments of despair, Our Blessed Mother appeared to him and said, "If you seek salvation, spread the Holy Rosary." The last forty years of his life were spent propagating the rosary. He is the one who built the national shrine of Our Lady of the Rosary in Pompeii, Italy. He died in 1926 and was beatified by Saint John Paul II in

October, 1980, the only former high priest of
the church of Satan ever to be beatified.

A Promise Kept

Louis Kazmirek, a layman and former
official escort for the International Pilgrim
Virgin Statue, (the statue that has been seen
to weep some twenty times) had made a
promise to the Blessed Virgin to say his
rosary every day of his life. Years later, in
the Air Force, having been up all night - 38
hours straight - working the shifts answering
the Red Cross calls, he dropped to his knees
dead tired. Alone in the empty barrack he
began to say his night prayers and suddenly
remembered that he hadn't said his promised
daily rosary. His conscience started working
but he thought: "Surely after all this, I'm
excused - the Blessed Mother will
understand." He looked up at his rosary,
wrapped securely around the post of the
headboard of his bunk where he habitually
wound it while away on duty. Though
feeling the prodding of his conscience, he cut
off his prayers and crawled into bed, totally

spent. "Mother," he thought, "if that one rosary means that much to you, let me know." As he was falling asleep he became aware of a light scraping sound and a thin metallic thud. He sat up and turned to the headboard - there was no rosary on the post; he found it, self-untangled, on the floor! He sprang from the bed, knelt down and prayed the most devout rosary of his life!

From the Popes

Did you know that between the year 1402 and the present there have been 502 papal pronouncements on the rosary? No other devotion has received as much papal approval and blessing. Saint John Paul II has said, "The rosary is my favorite prayer." He gave out hundreds of thousands of rosaries. St. Louis de Montfort claims that if you give someone a rosary or make one, or teach someone how to say it, you receive a special grace. Saint John Paul II probably figured that if he gave out a hundred thousand rosaries, he received a hundred thousand graces! It was noted that when he was at home, he would often lead the rosary himself on Vatican Radio. There have been many stories about bishops and cardinals going over to Rome and saying, "Holy Father, we have this problem in the diocese..." He would open his drawer and give them a rosary, saying, "This is the answer for all of your problems."

Before Saint John Paul II there was Pope John Paul I, pope for only thirty-three days and yet he left the plea, "Pray the rosary for peace." Prior to him was Pope Paul VI who, in 1965, wrote an encyclical in which he asked the people to pray the rosary. In 1967 he said, "Pray the rosary for world peace." Before him was John XXIII, pope from 1958 to 1963. He spoke out thirty-eight times on the power of the rosary. People are not aware that he wore the rosary around his neck and prayed fifteen decades every day (as did Pope Benedict XV). He called the rosary the "school of perfection in which you can acquire every virtue." Preceding him was Pope Pius XII who also said fifteen decades of the rosary every day.

Pius XI gave rosaries as wedding gifts. Pope St. Pius X said, "Of all the prayers, the rosary is the most beautiful and the richest in graces, the most pleasing to Mary. Love the rosary and recite it every day." Pope Leo XIII made sixteen pronouncements on the rosary and called it "the remedy of all evils and the root of all our blessings." Preceding him was Pius IX who is famous for saying "Give me an army to say the rosary and I will conquer the world." The story is told that one day while giving a tour of the Vatican to some of his friends, he was asked, "Holy Father, what's the greatest treasure in the Vatican? The Pieta (at that time worth $16 million), or the Sistine Chapel?" The pope reached into his pocket and pulled out his rosary and said, "This is the greatest treasure in the Vatican. Of all devotions, the rosary has produced the most miracles." And the Church is indebted to Pope St. Pius V who established the feast day of the Holy Rosary in thanksgiving for the great Christian victory over the Turkish fleet at Lepanto in 1571, which saved Christian civilization in Europe.

From the Saints

St. Clement Hoffbauer had the faith to believe he could convert the most hardened sinner if he devoutly prayed just one rosary for him. St. Francis de Sales said, "Next to the Mass, the rosary is the most powerful prayer when you meditate on the mysteries." In fact he prayed the rosary everyday for the return of Calvinists to the Catholic Church and in his lifetime he was instrumental in bringing 72,000 Calvinists back into the Catholic Faith. St. Francis de Sales said that were he able to retire from the world he would take with him his two greatest weapons, "my rosary and my pen."

A priest friend of St. Padre Pio knew that the stigmatist said about fifteen rosaries a day even though he was very busy with saying Mass, hearing confessions and giving spiritual direction. His friend asked if he had been able to say his fifteen rosaries yesterday. "Actually, a few more", he answered. "Did you say 20?" "Yes." His friend grew suspicious. "30?" "Yes." "50?" "Yes." "100?" "Yes." "150?" "Yes." "More?" "Yes, I said 160 rosaries yesterday." This is told by a priest who was an intimate friend of Padre Pio. (The question of how could he say 160 rosaries in one day - something humanly impossible - could be answered by considering that since he was known to have the gift of bilocation, he could say two at the same time! He had it a little bit easier than we do, but that's no reason why we should not say all we can!)

My own grandmother had a great love for the rosary. She died at the age of 93, completely deaf and almost blind. Since she could no longer read or watch TV she spent her time in her favorite chair saying maybe ten or twelve rosaries a day. She had a collection of all kinds of rosaries, some had big beads, some small, some colored and some odd-shaped. Sometimes she would make a point of "lecturing" to us and picking each one at a time would say something like, "Now, Francis, this one's for you; these pink ones

216

are for your sisters, and this one's for the pope and this wooden one's for the souls in Purgatory." She probably thought the pope was still Pius XII, since she hadn't heard any Vatican news in the past fifty years! She prayed these rosaries every day and was a great blessing to my family and to myself in particular. In fact, Bishop Sheen said that if you take care of someone who's elderly or handicapped, you will get special graces from God for your family. It's true. I have seen that in my own life.

XI. The Blessed Trinity and the Family

Jesus Mary and Joseph

Jesus, Mary and Joseph

Once lived in Galilee;

Mary loved Jesus

Who slumbered within her,

Mary loved Joseph of Galilee.

Joseph and Mary

Made God's Son a family.

Jesus, Mary and Joseph
Once stayed in Bethlehem;
Mary kissed Jesus

Who slumbered beside her,

Joseph knelt softly in Bethlehem:

He was her husband,

and he would take care of them.

Jesus, Mary and Joseph
Went home to Galilee;

Mary and Joseph

Watched Jesus with wonder,

As Jesus looked out from Galilee

Longing to add all Mankind

To his family . . .

The Blessed Trinity and the Family

Coincidental to the name in its title, *The Blessed Trinity and the Family*, this article has three sections: the mystery of the Blessed Trinity, the Holy Family of Jesus, Mary and Joseph as the reflection of the Blessed Trinity and Catholic Family Life in relation to the Blessed Trinity.

The Catholic religion is a religion of mysteries and the Blessed Trinity holds the supreme and ultimate place. The common understanding of the word 'mystery' is that of something to be solved, such as in the stories of Sherlock Holmes or Agatha Christie. There's a difference between a puzzle and a mystery: we solve a puzzle, but we enter into a mystery. For Catholics, a mystery is supernatural, a divinely revealed truth which refers to the order of God and his Grace. It so exceeds the capacity of the human mind that it cannot be fully understood. In other words, the mysteries of our Faith are not something we could have come up with on our own. They are not

219

manifest in the natural order of the world and therefore their existence must be revealed by God alone. The doctrine of the Blessed Trinity is not something that we could have known had not God revealed it through Sacred Scripture.

A sixth-grader once asked me: "What's the difference between magic and a mystery?" The answer holds the master key to a fundamental principle of the Catholic Faith: *seeing what is unseen*. Magic tricks the human mind to thinking something is there, but is actually not; *a mystery is so above the capabilities of the human mind that it can never be fully comprehended*. For example: after the magician says his magic words, it appears he is sawing the woman in half, but we know it actually is not happening. In the mystery of the Eucharist, after the priest's words of Consecration, it doesn't appear that anything happened, but by faith we know that Christ is actually present.

So a mystery is something that God manifests to us. And the definition goes on to say that the incomprehensibility of revealed mysteries derives from the fact that they are manifestations of God who is infinite, and therefore beyond the complete grasp of the human mind and intellect. Nevertheless, though incomprehensible, *mysteries are intelligible,* which means we can understand something about them. One of the primary duties of a believer is to grow in the Faith, and through prayer, study and experience to develop an understanding of what God has revealed.

The Holy Trinity

The word 'Trinity' first appeared around the year 200 A.D. and is the central doctrine of the Christian religion: that *there is one God only, yet three divine persons.* God who is one and unique in his infinite substance and nature exists in three distinct but inseparable persons: Father, Son and Holy Spirit. Each person - distinct but not separate from the other - is equal in dignity and identical in divinity, sharing the same divine power, attributes, mind and the will of the Divine nature. Each person is not the other, yet each remains the same God. God the Father is not God the Son; God the Son is not God the Holy Spirit; God the Holy Spirit is neither the Father nor the Son. The definition goes on to say that the one and only God as Father generates, begets, the Son from all eternity, and the Holy Spirit, from the mutual divine love of the Father and the Son, proceeds eternally as Divine Love from that union. The three divine persons are co-equal, co-eternal and consubstantial and deserve co-equal glory in adoration. Now *this* is what is called a Mystery!

Although this mystery of the Trinitarian God will ever be incomprehensible, it is, as stated above, intelligible, and here are some ways of entering into this primary mystery of the Catholic Faith.

Nature and Person.

A nature is *what* something is; a person is *who* someone is. Nature answers the question, "What?" Person answers the question, "Who?" So in God we know there is one divine *nature* or one divine essence yet three divine *persons,* each person totally possessing the divine nature.

The Shamrock. St. Patrick used the shamrock to teach children how there can be one God and yet three divine persons, by showing them the one plant with three different leaves.

H2O. And we've come a long way since the three-leaf clover! Bishop Sheen used the analogy of H_2O, which exists in the liquid form of water, ice or steam, showing one substance in three distinct forms. (These examples were contested once by a kid in my CCD class. He said, "Well, Father, there must be three gods, because one is Father, one is Son, one is Holy Spirit - one plus one plus one equals three!" Well, his math was right, but his answer was wrong. One god plus one god plus one god does make three gods, but the correct answer is one person plus one person plus one person equals one God!)

Now let's take a moment to consider how we can approach an understanding of this incredible, beautiful being who is Father, Son and Holy Spirit. First of all, the old expression "Me, Myself and I" can help here. When looking in a mirror, one can say, "That's *me* in the mirror"; then there is the *thought of myself* as seen in the mirror and then there is the *I* who is looking at *me* in the mirror and who is thinking of *myself* - a personal *three-in-one* situation! It could be said that from all eternity, God the Father sees his *Self*, and has an eternal *knowledge* of his *Self*, which, in the case of God, is a person, the one we call the Word of God, the son of God, the second person of the Blessed Trinity. Since the Father is a person, and his *Self* is a person, and since "God is Love", the third person of the Blessed Trinity is the love God has for himself. The union of the Son, knowing and loving the Father, and the Father, knowing and loving the Son, is also a person, the third person of the Blessed Trinity, the Holy Spirit. Bishop Sheen referred to the Father as the "thinker." From all eternity the Father reflects, and that one idea, that one image the Father has - divine and infinite - is the Son. He says the Father is the "thinker", the Son is the "thought", and the relationship, the bond between the "thinker" and the "thought" is *Love* – the Holy Spirit.

(The word *spirit* that Jesus used to explain the Holy Spirit seems to be drawn from the human experience known between two lovers, between husband and wife - the bond of love in the silence of eternity, where no word need be spoken, which is known as the "breath of the spirit", the "Ruah" or sigh, the sigh of love between the Father and the Son.)

We can know, through natural law and human reason, that God is one. However, the fact that God is three divine persons had to be revealed, and there are hints of this in Sacred Scripture. For example in the book of Genesis, God says, "Let *us* make man in *our* own image" (Gn 1:26). Some theologians see that as a glimpse of the fact that God is triune. But

with the New Testament the Blessed Trinity
is most perfectly revealed, beginning with the
Blessed Mother at the Annunciation, when
the angel Gabriel said to her, *"The Holy
Spirit will come upon you, the power of the
Most High will overshadow you, hence the
child to be born will be the Holy One of
God"* (Lk 1:35). The mystery of the Blessed
Trinity – God as Father, Son and Holy Spirit
- is revealed for the first time in human
history, followed up by several other
references in the Gospels:

"In the beginning was the Word. The Word
was with God and the Word was God."
(Jn 1:1)

At the Baptism of Jesus, when he came up
from the water, the *dove* came upon Him and
the *voice* from Heaven said, "This is my
beloved *Son*, in whom I am well pleased."
(Mt 3:17)

At the Transfiguration, when the three apostles saw Jesus overshadowed by a *cloud* and a *voice* was heard saying, "This is my beloved *Son*, listen to him." (Mk 9:7)

In John 16, Jesus says that he will send the Holy Spirit, and in John 14, he talks about the Father sending the Holy Spirit, and at the end of Matthew's gospel, we read, "Go out into the whole world and baptize in the name of the Father and of the Son and of the Holy Spirit."
(Mt 28:19)

(Notice the word used is not "names", for that would mean three gods, but "name", for one God, Father, Son and Holy Spirit.)

The Holy Family

The Holy Family has been called in church history the "Earthly Trinity" or the "Terrestrial Trinity", because St. Joseph, Our Lord and Our Lady seemed a logical, human reflection of the Blessed Trinity in heaven: Joseph, considered the mirror image or human portrait of God the Father, Jesus, being the actual Son of God, and Mary, known as the temple of the Holy Spirit.

St. Joseph

St. Joseph's role as head of the Holy Family is our closest *human* resemblance to God the Father next to Christ himself. Christ, as a divine person, had a human nature, as was stated above, but he is not a human person. St. Joseph has been called "the mirror of God the Father", the "shadow of the Father", the "reflection of God the Father". And in the lives of the saints there are beautiful references to Our Lord, then on earth, seeing in St. Joseph a reminder of his own divine Father in heaven.

228

Our Lord

As for Our Lord, we know he is actually the Incarnation of the Word of God; he is that *thought* that God the Father had from all eternity become incarnate. *"The Word became flesh and dwelt among us."* The Bible says he made his tabernacle among us; 'he pitched his tent' as the Greek phrase goes. When meditating on the Holy Family one can only marvel at the unbelievable reality of God living in that little house in Nazareth, God breathing, moving, eating, sleeping, spending day after common day working in the carpentry shop. What did they talk about, those other two, with their lives up close and touching divinity? How did they spend their time, they who had known the visits of angels and had now become the family of the only God, the seedbed of universal salvation? We of today can casually say "Emmanuel" - "God is with us" - and gaze upon him with blind eyes of faith. Would they too have whispered "Emmanuel" while gazing through the eyes of faith upon the human form of God?

229

Our Lady

And what about Our Lady? St. Paul refers to each Christian as a temple of the Holy Spirit, (with the option of becoming a shrine or a basilica or even a cathedral of the Holy Spirit if there is the will and the effort for true sanctity!) Our Lady has been called the "Temple of the Holy Spirit" as well, but should be seen as the *living* temple or tabernacle of the Spirit, to have a more adequate image of her. She is also called the "Spouse of the Holy Spirit" which is a much more accurate image, but even this title does not convey her true relationship with the Holy Spirit. St. Maximilian Kolbe in his theological writings called the Holy Spirit *the uncreated and eternal Immaculate Conception,* and at Lourdes, when Our Lady was asked by St. Bernadette who she was, she replied, "I am the Immaculate Conception." Maximilian Kolbe says she was using the name of her spouse and that it would be easier to separate light from the sun than it would be to separate Our Lady from

230

the Holy Spirit! He says that from the moment of Our Lady's creation in her mother's womb she was filled with the Holy Spirit and became his temple and dwelling place, but he goes further to say that Our Lady can actually be considered *the quasi-incarnation* of the Holy Spirit - not an actual *Incarnation* as is Jesus Christ of the second person of the Blessed Trinity, but a participation of personal, life-sharing union. Servant of God Frank Duff, founder of the Legion of Mary, in writing on this same subject, says that in heaven we will probably do a "double-take" when seeing the Holy Spirit and Mary - they will be so much alike!

Catholic families should have a special relationship with our Blessed Mother, because of that special relationship she has with each Person of the Blessed Trinity. She is the chosen daughter of God the Father, the mother of God the Son and spousal "self" of the Holy Spirit. No other human creature will ever know this relationship. So just as Our Lady has a special relationship with the

Blessed Trinity, so should the Catholic Family.

We know that the human being was created in the image of God, and by extension, it can be said that the family is intended to be an image of God, a reflection of the Blessed Trinity, a pattern for family life. What are some of the Trinitarian qualities that should be mirrored in the Catholic Family?

Love

The family is a reflection of the Blessed Trinity because it is a social unit, made up of social beings existing and relating as a community. The Blessed Trinity shows us a community of persons whose relationship is love. The individual human being is in the image and likeness of God from the standpoint that he can think and know and will live forever; the human family reflects the Trinity because it is intended to be a community, a community of love. St. Thomas Aquinas says there is total unselfishness and infinite giving in the

Blessed Trinity, but in families disunity and chaos grows when one person, or when each person seeks his own preferences instead of being generous and self-giving and being an individual of self-donation. St. Augustine has written, "A community is a multitude united by agreement about the things they love." Just as there is unconditional love between the Father, Son and Holy Spirit, so families are intended to strive for that divine ideal of unconditional love.

Life

God is love, God is life, the fullness of life, of truth, of beauty, and it should be the longed-for ideal of every Catholic parent to nurture these same qualities in themselves and in their children. God is the source of life, and that life is fruitful, begetting eternally his Son who, with his Father, eternally generates the Holy Spirit. The Blessed Trinity is not static, but forever fruitful. The Catholic Family, in the image of the Trinity, is called to fruitfulness, to the openness to new life, to the marvelous blessings of children.

Honor

In the 'family' of the Blessed Trinity, there is perfect harmony, perfect unity, perfect love. So the elements in the environment of Catholic family life should be love, honor and respect: parents honoring God directly and through their love for each other and their children; children learning and assimilating the virtues of honor and respect. I like to use what I call the "violin example". The Stradivarius is probably the most famous violin ever made, and the most valuable. Were someone, being aware of this, allowed to hold a Stradivarius, the reaction would be something like: "Wow! This is amazing! I'm touching something that must be worth a million dollars!" In imitation of the inner life of the Blessed Trinity it is a much greater kind of reverence than this that should be shown for one another as people made in the image and likeness of God, and as a Catholic family made to be a reflection of the Most Holy Trinity.

Contemplation

Theologians, in writing on the life of the persons in the Blessed Trinity, comment on the interacting *eternal contemplation* between each person with the other: the Father reflecting with love upon his *Self*, his Son, with love; his Son, reflecting upon the Father, with love; and that love between the two being the third person, the Holy Spirit - eternally contemplating the other two. (It's what the Blessed Trinity "does all day"!) Catholic Family life (also made up of persons!) should be arranged in some way to give praise and homage to the Blessed Trinity by creating a contemplative setting in the home, some regular time for quiet prayer and reflection, for example. Perhaps special reading times could be inserted into the week where restful, inspirational books would be shared. Perhaps there's room for a quiet prayer corner, outfitted with statue, crucifix, etc., and an assortment of good books for all ages, where members of the family can drop in and spend some contemplative time in solitude.

Generosity

Also to be considered in the Catholic Family's honoring of the Blessed Trinity is the virtue of generosity. We read in John 3:16, *"For God so loved the world that he gave his only Son."* That selflessness and generosity is the supreme example intended by God for all mankind to be thankful for, to appreciate, and to follow. Selflessness practiced by family members is a guarantee that God's blessings and graces will be available, especially when the crosses of life are laid upon them. Selfless generosity is the seedbed of family joy and respect, and the more it is evident in the home, the more is the Christian character developed in the children and matured in the adults. Yielding to another person's preference, whether reasonable or not, is one of the hardest things for human nature to endure, but when done with the intention of pleasing God in mind, is

236

the hallmark of a holy home and of a saintly family.

Harmony

In the Blessed Trinity is found the source of all unity, harmony and peace, which are the building blocks for all successful family life, especially Catholic Family life, where the Sacraments are frequented and the Gospel values are lived. There is an added dimension as well and that is *the calling to be instruments* of unity, harmony and peace, and not merely recipients of these valuable conditions. St. Francis of Assisi summed up this calling in his prayer:

"Lord, make me an instrument of your peace.
Where there is hatred, let me sow love.
Where there is injury, pardon.
Where there is sadness, joy."

This calling asks of family members to do what they can to be instruments of peace within the family, to reconcile, to forgive, to yield personal preference, to swallow pride, to hide the hurts - whatever it takes to instill that likeness to the Blessed Trinity in the home. A practical suggestion to help with this would be to get the St. Francis prayer holy card for each member of the family and perhaps occasionally - as before a meal or bedtime - read the prayer together. Some members may want to add it to their personal prayers, as well.

Another idea for peace in the home is the ceremony of the Enthronement of the Sacred Heart, when a family will install a statue or a picture of the Sacred Heart of Jesus in a prominent place in the home. This becomes a permanent reminder of the promises of Jesus, one of which is the promise that he will establish peace in the home that honors his Sacred Heart.

After all these lines and thoughts on the subject of the Most Holy Trinity, we find we are still left with mystery, the mystery of *how,* how God, in his eternal Being, can be One yet Three. We know he is not only the beginning and the source of all creation, but is the terminus, or end, of all creation. In general, he is the destiny of every faithful soul created, and, in particular, the ultimate goal and destination of the Catholic Family, which, in that future unending 'present', will be united forever in the ravishing view of the Beatific Vision of the Most Holy Trinity, where mystery is no more, *"for they shall see him as he is" (1 Jn 3:2).*

XII.   Ten Steps to Holiness

The Lover

You ask I not be saint for sainthood's sake,
nor crave the flavor of your daily bread,
to let *You* choose what portion I shall break
off penance's charred loaf: you'd see me fed

a hunger for starvation, when there comes

another hunger, tempting with its lie
of appetizing mold, its feast of crumbs!
Nor should I seek to sail Your still, starred
sky,

Your cloistered cloud . . . Upon earth's
steady plain,

with sown good soil about life's hidden roots,
You ask I thrive – bent twig! – upon Your
rain,
unbudded branch Your promise of love's
fruits!

And so I live by one inverted grace:
a lover, blind, in Love's unfelt embrace!

Ten Steps to Holiness

Everyone is familiar with the statement, *"You can't give what you don't have"*. When it comes to the great challenge for Catholic parents of instilling in their children the primary purpose of life - to know and love God, to choose his Will above all else - and the implanting in their lives and souls of a true desire for heaven, the need for personal holiness becomes paramount for both mother and father. With regard to spiritual development in the Catholic family, it has been said that if the parents are striving to live a life of sanctity, the spiritual life of the children will be good; if the parents are content with the level of mere goodness, the children will be spiritually indifferent; if the parents are spiritually indifferent, the children will be . . . ?

With these thoughts in mind I offer these ten steps to personal holiness as a spiritual checklist for the individual parent, with the suggestion that they periodically share their progress, with the goal of passing

241

on life spiritually to their children as they have already done biologically!

The French author Leon Bloy has written: *"There is only one tragedy in life - not to be a saint"*. Personal holiness is really the one thing in life that matters, the only purpose for human existence, not just for those of the true Faith but for every human being. For Catholic Christians, with a glorious history of sanctity in the lives of the saints, and with the availability of the sacraments, it is a reachable ideal, an attainable goal. Every person will die one day whether it be at twenty, fifty or eighty years of age; what will matter is the state of the soul. Will it be in the state of grace? Will it have God's life within it? Sanctifying Grace is the "life support system" for heaven - you can't live there without it! If our relationship with God is right, everything else will fall into place. Holiness is the requirement for relationship with God, because God *is* Holiness.

1) Desire the Goal. We must pray to desire holiness, pray to want it desperately. It

242

is not something that will come without effort and perseverance. True, it is a gift of God, as all things are, but to receive it there must be an honest yearning for it, like what was had by the saints who have shown the way. It should be as with anything in life, the goal longed for, the Grail so fervently sought. Imagine a pilot flying a plane with no goal and with little interest in seeking one. Eventually the fuel is gone and there is the inevitable crash. Life on earth is like that; without the goal of personal holiness, and the fuel of desire for deep love for God, there is always the inevitable crash. But the living of a holy life assures us of the proverbial safe landing.

2) **A Rule of Life.** Pursuing a life of holiness requires discipline and a plan, a schedule to keep prayerfully focused, and some kind of daily spiritual agenda or routine, custom-made to fit one's busy individual daily life. Cardinal Newman advised that, upon rising in the morning, first thoughts should be given to God; make the sign of the cross before the feet even hit the

floor and you're already on the way! There is the Morning Offering which makes a love-gift to God of our day and all it contains. To have it and other prayer cards stuck in the frame of the mirror is a good idea: while the hair is being combed, the heart is being offered.

O Jesus,
through the Immaculate Heart of Mary,
I offer Thee my prayers, works, joys and
sufferings of this day
for all the intentions of Thy Sacred Heart,
in union with the Holy Sacrifice of the Mass
throughout the world,
in reparation for my sins, for the intentions of
all our associates,
and in particular for the general intentions
recommended this month.

St. John Vianney has said it is God's way to give more than enough graces in the morning to last the whole day. Prayer in the morning is like breakfast: it keeps the body going for a long time. Prayer, in fact is real food for the soul, so the question is asked: could a man live on breakfast only for the rest of his life? This is really an important spiritual question, for if we're not praying three times a day - or at least morning and night - we're probably not getting the proper spiritual nutrition. We know what happens when a person stops praying for an extended period of time. There is retarded spiritual growth and the virtue God intends for the health of the soul will not develop. So the day begins with the Morning Offering and ends with an Examination of Conscience and Act of Contrition, the two "bookends" that keep the spiritual life upright! Other components that can be included in a lay person's Rule of Life, depending on individual circumstances, are daily Mass and Communion, the daily rosary alone or with the family, some quiet time (say, fifteen minutes) for "sitting with God", and some habit of short spiritual reading.

3) Mass and Holy Communion. Pope Pius X said there is no greater way to grow closer to Christ than to actually receive him in Holy Communion, and that the reception of the Holy Eucharist is the shortest, quickest, and most direct way to holiness. This is because the Eucharist *is* Jesus, the source of all grace, and grace is the source of all holiness. For the parent - or *parents,* if possible - to incorporate daily or frequent Mass and Holy Communion into their Rule of Life would be the securing of a treasury of graces for both personal and family life. There is the practice of a brief internal recollection period (a few minutes) before and after Holy Communion that enhances the reception of the sacrament.

4) Frequent Confession. I often tell the kids in my parish that going to confession is like giving their soul a shower, and since they take regular bodily showers they should at least shower their souls every week or so! I ask them, "What if I came to your home for dinner without having taken a shower in five or six years? You'd have me eating out in the garage!" Yet people do come to Mass and Communion, maybe not in the condition I just described, but needing a soul-shower nonetheless. Imagine some of the things that have built up in there after a long absence from confession - there would definitely be a need for a good cleansing! When one is preparing a Rule of Life, frequent confession is a building block, since spiritual direction and is often an un-looked-for benefit. Something to keep in mind is that confession is not just for the remission of sins, but can be a rich source of guidance and encouragement. The parents who find a friendly, understanding priest to go to periodically for confession, spiritual guidance and related life issues, have uncovered a rich treasure-vein of holiness.

5) One's State in Life. The "duties of our state in life" as the spiritual writers called them, afford built-in opportunities for personal holiness. If one were to follow the example of St. Therese, the Little Flower, these duties would be fulfilled with love. Regardless of the life-style, holiness is found in doing the little things in daily life from a motive of love for God. Changing a diaper or changing planes, doing dishes or doing ten laps, love is the proper attitude. If "little things mean a lot" in human relationships, they mean everything when it comes to the Divine, for so called "minor" things done with the maximum of love is sanctity.

The whole Theology of Work consists of this one point: the doing of the duties of our state in life to the very best of our ability, out of love for God and neighbor. Holiness is not the doing of extraordinary penances, or going as a missionary to foreign lands, performing miracles or experiencing ecstasy or levitation; true holiness is found in the ordinary things done extraordinarily well. Our state of life, with all it entails, is the custom-made setting God's providence has arranged for us to be sanctified in. There is no other. And in the state of marriage where "two become one", there is the added unique benefit of the sharing of the holiness of the spouse.

6) Spiritual Reading. Devotional reading and prayer are the two pillars of Catholic devotion; spiritual reading and study are the two channels of Catholic belief.

Parents will need to find some free time to deepen their knowledge of the Catholic Faith by reading from the rich collection of sources available, such as the scriptures, the life of Christ, the lives and writings of the saints. The more that can be known about God and what he does, the more will he be loved. Spiritual reading would primarily feature scripture, some reading of the Bible. There are inexpensive commentaries or Study Guides available; the use of a missal for daily reading is another source. To quote St. Jerome, "Ignorance of scripture is ignorance of Christ".

The lives of the saints are important because if any one thing has contributed to making saints it is people reading about them! And that's because people become what they contemplate. The boy who wants to become a great athlete will read and think about the great Stars of sports and desire to become like them. The lives of the Stars of the Catholic Church are there to be read and absorbed, for Catholics of all ages.

In addition to books there are recordings. Today there is probably no greater way of getting educated on one's own than with CDs and DVDs. The availability of these discs probably offers the greatest opportunity for growing in knowledge since the invention of the printing press. Literally thousands of titles on just about any subject, including classic and contemporary Catholic speakers and authors are available on CD. A working father can do "spiritual listening" of the Bible, for example, while sitting in traffic on the way home from work. A study at UCLA reported that the average person can gain two years of college education in three years of sitting in the car! So with a CD player in the car you've got a university on wheels! The car is also a good place for prayer and reflection, or reciting the rosary. It's a modern virtue to make this kind of use of driving time!

7) To Be an Apostle. Serving others is another means of growing in holiness, and it has the by-product of giving us a sense of spiritual and social well-being. Visiting someone in the nursing home or teaching children the Catechism boosts the spirit and sharpens our sense of charity. I have often found that the most miserable people in life are the ones who never serve other people. The secret of happiness lies in not thinking of ourselves, but of others. This is something not just for the parents alone on their spiritual journey, but is a value for their children as well, a value I have seen take root and blossom in many young lives as members of the Junior Legion of Mary. And the deeper meaning of service is found in Matthew: *"When I was hungry you fed me, when I was thirsty you gave me a drink, when I was sick or in prison you visited me. . . " (Mt 25:35).* It is a *reality* that it is *actually Jesus himself* we serve in our acts of charity because he continues his life in human beings through his Mystical Body, which is a *real* Presence. Our final destiny will depend on how we treat others. It will be a great day when, coming before Jesus and hearing him say, "Thank you for visiting me when I was ill; thank you for loving and

teaching me when I was a little child; thank
you for your patient tolerance of me when I
was a troubled soul. Come receive the
everlasting life prepared for you."

8) The Use of Sacramentals.
Sanctifying grace comes primarily to us
through the seven sacraments, but there are
also special graces given through the use of
sacramentals blessed by the Church. The
crucifix, holy water, the rosary, scapular,
miraculous medal, statues and holy cards are
very effective means of bringing ourselves
and others closer to God. In times of
temptation many saints found consolation
and encouragement by meditating on the
crucifix, a reminder of the passion and death
of Christ. Blessing oneself with holy water
with the intention of sorrow for sin can
remove venial sin from the soul. It can also
be given to people as a safeguard against evil
influences. Religious medals and holy cards
carry much spiritual power: I remember one
college student who began attending daily
Mass after accepting and reading a prayer on
Holy Communion!

252

As for the miraculous medal, it got its name because of the many miracles that occur as a result of wearing it. There is the remarkable story of Alphonse Ratisbon, an atheistic Jew who, after accepting a miraculous medal, was instantly converted, received an infusion of the gift of faith, was baptized, became a priest, and started an order of priests in the Holy Land for the conversion of Jews. This of course was a major miracle through the use of the medal, but many "minor" miracles can happen as the apostolic Catholic begins to use them in works of service.

9) Devotion to Mary. Jesus *is* holiness; by sanctifying grace his life is in us; he is our interior life. Mary, being the mother of Jesus, is, therefore, the mother of our interior life. No saint in the Church was ever without some devotion to her, and a parent desiring to be holy must have some awareness of her and a personal devotion to her, since she was the "parent par excellence" in God's home at Nazareth. The simplest and most effective of all Marian devotions is St.

253

Louis de Montfort's *True Devotion to Jesus through Mary* (See Chapter VIII: *St. Louis de Montfort and the Family*). True Devotion basically means the giving over of ourselves, body, soul and spirit, to Jesus through Mary. It is the abandonment into her care of all that we have, are, and own: our life and all it holds, past, present, and future. It consists of two things: an actual consecration and the subsequent striving to live out that consecration in union with her, so as to be transformed into Jesus - which is the purpose of Christian life on earth. The Incarnation was brought about by Mary and the Holy Spirit who formed Jesus in her womb; Mary, in cooperation with the Holy Spirit, continues to form Christ in souls today. This was Mary's role then and it is Mary's role now; there can be no true holiness without her.

10) Acceptance of the Cross. Trials, disappointments, pain and suffering are a part of every life. Suffering, in and of itself, is morally neutral: it can lead a person closer to God or away from him, make one bitter or better, be a stepping stone or stumbling block to sanctity. Whenever suffering enters a life it should be remembered that it is the all-knowing permissive Will of God; he allows it for the purpose of perfecting or correcting the *life of the soul which lives forever.* He does not interfere with human nature (by working countless daily healing miracles) but has allowed it total freedom to be itself. It is "Tough Love" on God's part to see his children suffer, but in his wisdom he knows - however serious the cross - it is nothing compared with the spiritual, eternal pleasure and joy that is in store for the sufferer, *even while enduring the suffering itself,* as we're told the saints have experienced. Burning with love for God and aware of the great value of suffering, the saints willingly underwent great torments with a sense of joy for having been chosen to suffer in union with Christ. In addition, they would add fasting, mortification, prayer vigils, and other penances to show their love for him and to win the conversion of sinners. Parents of today may not have access to the great graces given to the saints of old, but they do possess the graces found in marriage and parenting, where trial, disappointment, problems, pain and suffering are always in the wings, waiting to spring on the stage of daily family life. It is high virtue to rely on the graces of marriage and parenting, which give insight into the crosses that come, and strength to endure their threatening shadows and debilitating weight. Victor Frankl once wrote that when suffering has meaning it becomes bearable. A woman suffering the pains of birth knows the meaning of her pain: to bring new life into the world. Christians, living in Christ's Mystical Body, know the meaning of their suffering. When it is accepted in a Christ-like way and united to Christ's sacrificial death on the cross, it becomes redemptive and sanctifying, and can be offered for their own loved ones and family, for the conversion of sinners, the souls in purgatory, or in reparation for sin.

Parents can be the saints God intends them to be: with a sincere desire to become holy, with a genuine love for God and a selfless acceptance of his Will, they will be

as ready as any saint to enter heaven, for
when holiness is sincerely sought, everything
becomes a grace.

XIII.   An Invitation

Life is for Learning

Life is for learning
Lesson of old,
The Greatest Story
Tongue ever told;
There is no knowledge
To match its worth:
Life is for learning
God came to earth!

Life is for learning
God's Holy Word,
Through all creation
He can be heard;
Life holds one message
Sent from above:
Life is for learning
To live by love.

Life is for learning
God's Golden rule,
Of all earth's wisdom
The crowning jewel!

Life holds one treasure
That can't be priced:
Life is for learning
The love of Christ!
Life is for living
the life of Christ!

An Invitation

A young Catholic woman was dating a young Protestant man who was much liked by the family and whom she was most interested in, but couldn't see herself married to him because he wasn't Catholic. So she asked her mother, "Mom, I can't make up my mind; would you start praying for James to become a Catholic?"

Her mother said, "Yes, Yes, I'll start praying right
away! I'll start a novena for him that he becomes a Catholic!"

A few months went by and the daughter said, "Mom, it's working! He's begun attending Mass with me!"

Her mother said, "Oh, this is terrific. We'll spread the word, asking for prayers, and I'll have a Mass said for his conversion. God willing, he'll see the light!"

A few weeks later the daughter said, "Mom, keep up the prayers! He's seeing Father Murphy and is taking instructions in the Faith!"

The mother exclaimed, "This is terrific! We'll really pour it on now! I'll get the nuns to pray!"

A couple of weeks went by and the daughter came rushing home crying, "Mom, stop the novena! Stop the prayers! Stop the nuns from praying!"

The mother said, "Why? What's wrong?"

"He thinks he wants to be a priest!"

This book, of course, focuses on Catholic marriage, Catholic parenting and Catholic family life, and I am well aware that some Catholic marriages are, as it were, "half-Catholic", with one of the spouses being of another religion. This is not to suggest that these "mixed" Christian marriages are inferior to the "fully Catholic" ones, or that they have not been included in my thinking while preparing this book. Not at all! It is to you, non-Catholic spouse married to a Roman Catholic, that I extend a sincere and open invitation to consider looking into the Catholic religion - not from

the idea of getting more Catholic converts, or
to make the marriage "fully Catholic" - but
from the view of deepening your *spiritual*
life, a richer awareness God's power and
presence; which would also benefit the soul
of your spouse. This capacity for spiritual
awareness of him is something God has given
to every human being, regardless of their
practice of or outlook on religion, as you
have probably already experienced in your
Christian life. In keeping with this invitation,
I'd like to first have you be aware of how
many things we Christians - Catholic and
Protestant - have in common. (I am not
unaware of spouses who are attached to no
denomination; and I hope you will consider
reading along these lines as well.) What do
we Catholics have in common with our other
brothers and sisters in Christ? Together we
believe:

in one God - Father, Son and Holy Spirit;

we believe in the Trinity - that God is one,
yet three divine persons - Father, Son and
Holy Spirit;

that Jesus Christ is the second person of the
Trinity;

that he became man through the Incarnation;

that he is our personal Lord and Savior;

that Jesus died on the cross for each one of
us;

that he rose from the dead and ascended into
Heaven;

that Jesus opened the gates of Heaven;

that he now sits at the right hand of the
Father;

that he will come again to judge the living
and the dead;.

that there is a Heaven and a Hell;

that the Bible is the inspired, infallible,
inerrant Word of God;

we believe in the Ten Commandments,

the Beatitudes,

the teachings of Christ,

Baptism and Matrimony,

the importance of daily prayer,

the importance of reading sacred scripture,

daily devotions, and a common respect for
the sanctity of human life.

Someone has said that the mind is like a parachute - it works best when it's open! I would ask you to pray to the Holy Spirit to open your mind and heart to *our* God who is goodness, beauty and truth. It is my prayer that I am able to unfold for you some of the beauty of Catholicism - the religion which holds so much of what you believe and love - the fact of which to now has probably been unknown to you.

I present here five "rooms", so to speak, of beauty and truth in the Catholic Religion, and I would like you to enter into these rooms with me, keeping in mind the title of this chapter - *An Invitation,* not a *solicitation!* Should the Holy Spirit ever inspire you to look further into the Catholic Church, these are the main "rooms" you would visit first:

The Sacraments,
Mary and the Saints,
Church History,
The Church and the Bible,
Moral Teachings.

Our first room contains the **Seven Sacraments,** which the Lord intended his followers to have, because they are the streams of grace that flow from the cross of Christ; they help us to build a more real, personal and intimate relationship with our Lord and Savior, Jesus Christ. All seven sacraments are found in the Catholic Faith: Baptism, Holy Eucharist, Confession, Confirmation, Matrimony, Holy Orders and Anointing of the Sick. Some denominations have two of these sacraments, some have more. What is a sacrament? The catechism answers: "A sacrament is a visible sign instituted by Christ to give us grace." Of the seven sacraments established by Christ, I'll highlight just a few. First, of course, is his greatest miracle, the Holy Eucharist. Holy Communion, we believe, is the true Body, Blood, Soul and Divinity of Jesus Christ under the appearances of bread and wine, Jesus truly present in his glorified, resurrected Body.

Dr. Scott Hahn, a noted Protestant convert to the Catholic Faith, says that for thirty years as a Protestant minister he loved the Lord as he found him in his beloved Bible, and that when he read the Bible it was like reading the "menu" of all the spiritual food God had prepared for mankind. On becoming Catholic, he realized that not only could he read the "menu" but he could actually partake of the Banquet itself! He could receive the Lord of the Bible in Holy Communion any day he chose! Scott Hahn understood that Jesus intended his words at the Last Supper - *This is my body, this is the cup of my blood* - to mean exactly what he said, for Jesus is God, Eternal Son of the Father, the second person of the Blessed Trinity, who can neither deceive nor be deceived.

In John Chapter 6 - Jesus' longest teaching in scripture - he repeats this teaching six times: *"My Flesh is true food and my Blood is true drink" (Jn 6:55). "Unless you eat the flesh of the Son of Man and drink his Blood you do not have life within you" (Jn 6:53). "The Bread that I will give is my Flesh for the life of the world" (Jn 6:51).*

On hearing this last pronouncement many disciples left him, shaking their heads at such a "hard saying." He let them go. Being Truth himself, he could not modify for them the truth of the gift of himself in the Holy Eucharist. This was his greatest miracle. It is called Transubstantiation: bread and wine become the living, glorified body and blood of Jesus. There are other events recorded in scripture where, when Jesus spoke, and his words took immediate effect: when at his cry, *"Lazarus come forth!"* *(Jn 11:43)* and a dead man came out of a tomb; when the demons obeyed his commands, and when his voice calmed the storm at sea.

Of other miracles in the Bible, I'd like to call your attention to some in particular which pertain to the great on-going miracle of the Eucharist:

The Multiplication of the Loaves
The Wedding Feast at Cana
The Walking on the Water
The Resurrection from Death

267

The Way to Emmaus

When Jesus fed the many thousands
with a few loaves, he showed his power over
bread;
at the wedding feast, where water became
wine, he showed his power over wine; when
he walked on water and rose from the dead
he showed he had power over his body; when
he walked along with the disciples he was
really present - but in disguise; and when
Jesus spoke at the Last Supper it was as if all
these miracles were rolled into one! The
Apostles had witnessed the miracles of the
bread and wine, had seen him walking on the
water - so they could believe and marvel at
the reality of his presence offered to them in
the "disguise" of bread and wine!

This great miracle occurs at every
Catholic Mass: Christ becomes truly present
under the appearances of bread and wine. By
the way, the Mass is another "room" I'd like
you to visit
sometime. Catholics believe there is only one
sacrifice, that Christ died once for all. The

Mass is not a new sacrifice, it is *the one and the same sacrifice of Christ made present here and now,* time and space being pushed aside as we are made present at a *re-presentation* of the one offering of himself on Calvary.

The companion sacrament to the Holy Eucharist is **Confession, or Reconciliation,** the forgiving of sins committed after Baptism. Jesus gave the authority to forgive sin to his Apostles when he breathed on them and said, "*As the Father has sent me so I send you . . . Receive the Holy Spirit. Whose sins you forgive are forgiven them and whose sins you retain are retained*" *(Jn 20:21-23).* Since the Catholic priesthood is linked directly and uninterruptedly to Christ through the Bishops, as successors to the first Apostles, that power to forgive sin given to the apostles is in turn passed on, through the laying on of hands by the Bishops, to the Catholic priest of today. The sacrament of **Holy Orders,** bestowed on the priest at Ordination, makes him an *Alter Christus* (the presence of Christ) when he administers the sacraments, so that in confession the sin is actually confessed to and heard by Christ himself present in the priest. The priest is merely the instrument and it is Jesus, God himself, who forgives the sin.

There is one other sacrament I would like to mention: the **Anointing of the Sick.** I think it is one of the best reasons to be Catholic! *"Is there anyone sick among you let him send for the priests of the Church. Let the priest pray over them anointing them with oil. If they have committed any sins their sins will be forgiven of them" (Ja 5:14-15).* What a wonderful sacrament this is that we can prepare our souls to enter eternal life, to be anointed when we are in serious illness or close to death.

The second room I invite you to visit is **Mary and the Saints;** once in this room awhile you will become conscious of a unique beauty and peace. There will be a sense of family, for the motherhood of Mary - her Motherhood of Christ and her motherhood of Christians - will be evident.

The title, "Mother of God"merely means that her son, Jesus Christ is Lord and God. And because Mary gave birth to Jesus Christ, who is Lord and God, she is truly God's mother. Bishop Sheen once asked, "If you could have created your own mother, wouldn't you have made her pure, beautiful, and as holy as could be imagined?" God is the only one who pre-existed his mother and being God, he had every right to make her perfect!

Saint Paul tells us of Christ, the second Adam. In God's providence, with this second Adam there would be a second Eve. Just as the first Adam and Eve were created by God without sin, so the new Adam, Christ, would have no sin: he would be the blameless one, he would be the sinless one. And the new Eve too would be created without sin. It is called Mary's Immaculate Conception, which means that the foreseen redeeming merits of Christ were applied to Mary at the moment of her conception. By *Anticipation* Mary was redeemed and saved by the grace of Christ when the merits of his passion, death and resurrection were applied to her. She was preserved from being tainted by the Original Sin, and she sings in her Magnificat, *"My spirit rejoices in God my* Savior!" We take the Angel Gabriel at his word when he called her "Full of Grace", the beautiful phrase that indicates a completed act that Mary was made full of grace from the first moment of her existence.

The role of Mary has been compared to the Ark of the Covenant in the Old Testament, which held the most sacred possessions of God's chosen people. The Ark was respected, honored and revered but never worshiped. Mary is the Ark of the New Covenant because for nine months she contained the Messiah within her womb, and carried him within her to her cousin Elizabeth, where, in the New Testament, the unborn babe, John the Baptist, leapt for joy in his mother's womb, just as David, in the Old Testament, leapt and danced as the Ark of the

Covenant came into his presence. Mary is the Ark of the New Covenant, and is respected, honored and revered by Catholics - but never worshiped!

It is, of course, the custom for most Christians to go to Christ directly. Many Catholics do that also, but many - because of her unique closeness to Christ - choose to go with Mary to Jesus. One reason for this is her power of intercession. At the Wedding Feast of Cana, when she asked him to do what would be his first miracle, he said, *"My hour has not yet come," (Jn 2:4)* but at her request changed water into wine. She should be considered an intercessor with him, for as he is mediator between us and the Father, she is mediator between us and Christ. She is our prayer-partner when we go to Jesus. The Bible says, *"The fervent prayer of a righteous man is very powerful" (Ja 5:16).* Who would be more righteous than his own Mother, the sinless one, the chosen vessel through which the Messiah would come into the world? Because Mary is the Mother of Jesus, who is God, she is the mother of all Christians, because of their participation in the life of Jesus. Because Christ lives within Christians, Mary is their spiritual Mother, just as she is Jesus' physical mother. At the foot of the cross Jesus said to John the beloved disciple, *"Behold your Mother" (Jn 19:27)*. She was his dying gift to mankind. Christians accept Christ as their personal Lord and Savior just as Mary did. Just as the angel told Joseph not to fear to accept Mary as his wife, so all Christians should have no fear or hesitation to accept her as their spiritual Mother. It's a most natural - and supernatural! - thing to do!

In Cooperstown, New York can be found statues, photos and memorabilia of the great baseball players; for football it's Canton, Ohio where the Football Hall of Fame is located. In the Catholic religion, God's closest friends are the saints, and they're enshrined in what I like to call the "Christian Hall of Fame" where we honor and respect those who lived Christ-like lives: individuals like Peter and Paul, Francis, Patrick, Theresa and thousands of other canonized saints. They are God's role models for all to see. Their images or pictures never receive "hero-worship" but they do deserve respect, honor and devotion. The Bible says, *"Honor your Father and Mother" (Ex 20:12)*. Certainly Jesus would have honored his Mother, so we honor and respect her as well.

I like to think of the Catholic Church as a family: God our Heavenly Father, Jesus our Savior, Lord and Brother; Mary our Mother, the angels and saints are our big sisters and brothers, or spiritual cousins - all to be counted on for help when needed. They are "our friends in high places!" or the cloud of witnesses that the Letter to the Hebrews speaks about. When one strolls through my "Christian Hall of Fame" in the Catholic Church, these many saints will recall what the Lord said about the tree being known by its fruit: a Saint Maximilian Kolbe, who gave his life in exchange for a prisoner in a Nazi concentration camp; a Maria Goretti, who died to preserve her virtue of chastity; a Mother Theresa, who unselfishly served the poorest of the poor. These are some of the fruits of the tree, Christians who have been baptized, nourished by the real presence of Christ in the Eucharist, forgiven in Confession, and strengthened by the sacrament of **Confirmation.**

Room number three for my Christian visitor's look into the Catholic Faith is **Church History.** Cardinal John Henry Newman, the famous convert from the Anglican Church once said, "to study history is to become Catholic". My intention here is to state objectively a brief overview of Catholic history with no intention of "selling" the Catholic Religion. It is necessary that these points be stated in order to give an honest exposition of what is believed by Catholic Christians.

Christ founded the Catholic Church upon Peter and the apostles two thousand years ago. Peter was the first Pope. Search "List of Popes" on the internet and up comes the unbroken line of two hundred and sixty-six Popes from Saint Peter to Pope Francis. Traditionally, the Bishops elect a successor upon the death of a Pope. When Peter died, Linus was elected pope; then Cletus, Clement, Sixtus, all the way down to Pope Francis. In a rare, but not unprecedented decision, Pope Benedict XVI resigned the papacy in 2013 due to health reasons.

In Matthew Chapter 16, we find Jesus saying to Peter in Aramaic, *"You are Peter (Kepha, meaning rock) and upon this rock (Kepha), I will build my Church and the gates of the netherworld shall not prevail against it. I will give to you (Peter) the keys of the Kingdom of Heaven. Whatever you bind on earth shall be bound in heaven and whatever you loose on earth shall be loosed in heaven"* (Mt 16:18-19).

It is inspiring to note that each of the first thirty Popes from the time of Saint Peter until the year 315 gave their lives as martyrs for their faith in our Lord and Savior, Jesus Christ.

It is true that throughout history, there have been several bad Popes, perhaps five or six out of the two hundred and sixty-five. But an

interesting note about this is that, even
though these men lived sinful or far from
saintly lives, they never taught error on issues
of faith and morals. The Holy Spirit
protected them from teaching error when they
spoke to the whole Church as Pope - with the
authority of Peter the "Rock".

Through the early centuries problems
arose in the Church, and there were abuses
with certain Church practices, but the Church
through the grace of God was able to reform
itself in the
Catholic Reformation, which began during
the Protestant Reformation and continued
after it. Unfortunately, the Protestant
reformers broke away from the Church and
eventually began their
own versions of what they felt the Church
should be. Martin Luther, Henry VIII,
Calvin, Knox,
Zwingli, Wesley, all "protested" to the
troubled state of the Church and attracted
followers, and soon many other "Churches"
were formed until now, when there are over
35,000 different denominations in America

alone. But the Bible relates that at the Last Supper Christ prayed that his disciples would be one. So we believe that the Catholic Faith was founded by a divine person: Jesus Christ who the Son of God. It can't be called a "man-made religion" because it wasn't begun by a man, as happened in the 1300s, 1500s or 1700s. It was founded by Jesus Christ, the Son of God.

The Catholic Church is both human and divine. It has a divine origin because it was founded by the God-Man Jesus Christ, and it is human because he left it in the hands of weak human beings. That's why the Church will always be in need of reform - because it is made up of imperfect members, because it is a Church of sinners. Look at the twelve apostles: Peter denied Christ three times, Judas betrayed him, and all of them abandoned him in the Garden of Gethsemane. Only one, John, stood at the foot of the cross. So the Church has had to endure immoral Popes, Bishops, priests, nuns and laity - sinners all! - but the Holy Spirit ever protects, preserves and renews it on its earthly journey heavenward.

The Catholic Church is identified by its fourfold character: it is One, Holy, Catholic and Apostolic. It is One because we have one Lord, one faith, one baptism, one founder Jesus Christ, one spiritual leader the Pope and one universal prayer, the Mass, said in a variety of liturgical expressions. The Church is Holy because it was founded by Christ, the Son of God and teaches his holy truths; it provides the sacraments which are the channels of sanctity; it has produced countless saints in the lives of holy men and women of its history from the very beginning.

The true Church of Christ is Catholic. It has a universal existence, in every country of the world and is open to all.

And it is Apostolic; it can trace itself back past the 1500s, past the 1200s, directly back to Christ and the twelve Apostles. Beginning with Peter there is an unbroken succession of Popes, ordained bishops and priests right up to the present day.

These four qualities of the Church
have attracted many people to become
Catholics through the years, but it is this last
one, the Apostolic history, that has been the
impetus in the last few years for many
Protestants to enter the Catholic Church. It
may not be too widely known that since 1993
four hundred Anglican priests from around
the world have entered the Catholic Church.
Also, in America, over 600 Protestant
ministers have become Catholic in the last
twenty years. What has been so inspiring for
these Protestant ministers, as they studied the
history of the early Church from the original
sources, is the writings of the early Church
Fathers, men like Ignatius, Irenaeus, Polycarp
and others. In their desire to be more one
with the primitive Church they discovered
and were more and more astounded to find
that the early gospel Church was Catholic in
its beliefs and practices. As they studied the
works of these early writers they came across
the *real presence of Christ in the Eucharist,
the Mass as a sacrifice, apostolic succession,
the liturgy, praying for the deceased, the*

primacy of the Bishop of Rome, the necessity of work, the importance of honoring the saints. It was the discovery that the Catholic Church today is the same as the original Church in the Bible, founded by Christ. There followed for these ministers the natural discovery of the development of doctrine: the acorn had now become the tree, and the Church of today, they realized, had the same teachings as in the beginning, with a fuller understanding of them. They learned there are no new doctrines and all public revelation ended with the death of the last apostle.

The fourth room I think you will be very comfortable in - it's the "Scripture Room", **The Church and the Bible.** The Catholic Church loves the Bible! It is the inspired Word of God! The Church encourages us to read the Bible. In fact, if you attended Catholic Mass every Sunday for three years you would hear almost the entire Bible in that three year cycle. If you went to daily Mass you would hear almost the entire Bible in a two year cycle.

What is the Catholic Church's relationship to the Bible? The Church is the Mother, not the daughter of the Bible. There was a Church before there was a Bible. It was the early members of the Church, under the inspiration of the Holy Spirit, who wrote the New Testament, the Letters, the Gospels, and it was the Church that compiled them.

Nowhere is it written that Jesus told the Apostles to write anything down. He commissioned them to preach the Good News to all creation and to baptize. This apostolic tradition was eventually written down, with some of it being passed on orally, but it was the Church of his Apostles and disciples that wrote the New Testament and compiled the Bible into the book that exists today. Just as in America the Founding Fathers wrote the Constitution and the Declaration of Independence, so Christ's 'Founding Fathers', the apostles and their successors, wrote down what became the sacred scriptures. In America our Constitution is interpreted by the Supreme Court; and the all-knowing Christ planned and established an interpreter for sacred scripture as well, and that, of course, is the Church he initially founded - the Church, author of sacred scripture. The question can be asked: How were the Christians saved in the first four hundred years of Christianity, when there was no complete Bible, when the random sacred books were not yet compiled into one volume? For at that time there *were fifty* Gospels in circulation with titles like the *Gospel of Thomas,* the *Gospel of Peter, the Acts of Pontius Pilate!* It was the Church of Rome, under the guidance of the Holy Spirit, that determined which of these Gospels was the inspired Word of God. In the year 393 all the bishops of Northern Africa gathered at the Council of Hippo to determine the 'Canon' of the Bible, the list of inspired books, and in 397 this was confirmed by them at the Council of Carthage. Martin Luther acknowledged this, writing that *"We are obliged to yield many things to the Papists, that with them is the word of God, which we received from them; otherwise we would have known nothing at all about it."*

284

(Luther's Sermon on John 16). (By the way, there is the old accusation that the Catholic Church did not want the Bible read by the people and used to chain it in the monasteries and churches so no one would get at it. The reason for the chaining, of course, is the same as every university had for chaining their valuable books so nobody would steal them. It's the same reason today why that little pen is chained at the teller's counter at the bank, or why that phone book is chained in the phone booth! Naturally it is not to keep it away from people, but to make it always available to everyone.)

Is the scripture the sole source of authority? We believe that the Bible is authoritative but is not the sole source of the teaching authority of Christ. How do we know what is the pillar and foundation of truth? What does the Bible say? Saint Paul says, *"God's household, the church of the living God, the pillar and bulwark of truth"* *(1 Tm 3:15)*. The Bible does not tell us which books are inspired by God, nor does it include in itself a table of contents. It is the

Church that affirms which books are inspired and which interpretations are correct. It is like students taking a class and not understanding the meaning of something written in the textbook; the teacher will be asked for the clarifying explanation of the text. So it is with the Bible and the Church. As we know, the Protestant Reformation was built on the beliefs of *Scripture Alone* and *Faith Alone.* Luther and others said that these were the pillars of the Reformation. The irony of this - the belief that 'Scripture alone' and 'Faith alone' are the only authority - is that it is not scriptural: it can't be found in the Bible. Paul wrote, *"Stand firm and hold fast to the <u>traditions</u> that you were taught, either by an oral statement or by a letter of ours" (2 Th 2:15).* The Reformers, in their zeal, left behind *Sacred Tradition* and kept only the written Word of God.

The other pillar of the reformation is 'Faith alone'. But it must be pointed out that this also cannot be found in the Bible, whereas its opposite can be. For example, in James is found, *"See how a person is justified*

by works and not by faith alone" (Ja 2:24).
St. Paul wrote in First Corinthians, *"If I have all faith so as to move mountains but do not have love, I am nothing"(1 Cor 13:2).* In Matthew Jesus said, *"For I was hungry and you gave me food, I was thirsty and you gave me drink" (Mt 25:35).* Our salvation depends on more than faith alone. Faith is necessary. Faith is vital. We are saved by faith, but not by faith alone. Paul says, *"Work out your salvation with fear and trembling" (Phil 2:12).* So the Bible tells us that believing in Jesus and his teachings is not enough; there must be work. *"If you love me, keep my commandments" (Jn 14:15).*

We Catholics believe that salvation comes by grace, by the Passion, Death and Resurrection of Christ applied to our life. We cannot save ourselves. Heaven is an eternal, supernatural destination and supernatural means are necessary to attain it, and only Christ can give them. We believe we are saved by the grace of Christ that works in our lives through faith, hope and charity. And so we follow the commandments. The Bible says even the devil has faith. The devil believes in God, but he is not saved because he does not have charity. So we are saved by the grace of Christ, but we want to cooperate fully with the grace and say yes to it. We have free will. We can accept the grace of Christ or - unfortunately -- we can reject the grace of Christ.

The one last thought about the relationship of the Catholic Church to the Bible is that the Catholic Church takes the Bible at face value, at its word, as when Jesus said, *"This is My Body. . . this is My Blood of the Covenant . . ." (Mt 26:26-27)*. It takes Jesus at his word in the Gospels: *"I was hungry, I was thirsty . . . "(Mt 25:35);* when he says, *"No one can enter the Kingdom of God without being born of water and Spirit" (Jn 3:5); "Unless you eat the flesh of the son of Man and drink his blood you shall not have life in you" (Jn 6:53). "Hail, favored one, the Lord is with you" (Lk 1:28). Most blessed are you among women" (Lk 1:42). "Whose sins you forgive are forgiven them"*

288

(Jn 20:23). "You are Peter and upon this rock I will build my Church" (Mt 16:18). These are some of the words of God himself that are taken literally, at face value, as true by the Catholic Church and cherished in the Holy Bible. We have now come to the last room in your visit to the Catholic Church. It is the "Living Room", the room of **Moral Teachings.** The Catholic Church has not watered down the difficult teachings of Christ on issues of faith and morals through all two thousand years of its existence. It can point to consistent respect for the sanctity of human life, from the moment of conception until natural death, especially today, when it is the clearest voice in the world in defense of the unborn, the elderly, the handicapped. It presents to the world the integrity of its teaching that it is always wrong to take innocent human life, whether it be in the womb or in a nursing home. It acknowledges that life is sacred from the moment of conception from the divine revelation of the unborn John the Baptist, who leapt in his mother's womb as he recognized the presence

289

of the unborn Jesus living in the womb of Mary.

The Catholic Church has continued to remain consistent in its upholding of the difficult moral teachings on divorce and remarriage. From the Bible we learn, *"Whoever divorces his wife and marries another commits adultery against her" (Mk 10:11).* The Catholic Church has remained true to the other teachings of sacred scripture on the difficult subjects, such as homosexuality, premarital sex and suicide. There are other moral issues too that can be found and derived from sacred scripture; for example, the condemnation of contraception as intrinsically evil, as immoral. Of all the Churches in existence today, only the Catholic Church has continued to teach Biblical truths about sexuality, marriage, and God's plan for married couples; the immorality of the culture of today in such things as homosexual activity, premarital sex, contraception, suicide, euthanasia, abortion, embryonic stem cell research, cloning, in vitro fertilization. Because it is founded by

Christ and protected through time by the Holy Spirit, the Catholic Church will not teach error on issues of faith and morals. Other denominations may change their beliefs to suit contemporary culture, or disregard sacred scripture to appease public pressure, but the Catholic Church has remained steadfast even on these unpopular teachings. And as we head into the future with additional bio-technological advances emerging, the steadfast Catholic Church will be more and more in the forefront as it confronts the evils that may arise. (In this connection, I recommend the prophetic works *Humanae Vitae*, the Church's document on human life, and the *Gospel of Life by* Saint John Paul II).

Should you feel, at this point in my "Invitation" (or perhaps later on) an inclination to look further into the Catholic Faith, or have some misgivings about the possibility of even taking such action on such a serious matter, there is something you should be aware of, something I think would help, that could put you more at ease; and that is *you would not be alone, you would*

not be the only one: it is what the Holy Spirit has been doing in recent years in the Catholic Church.

If you were to go on the internet and search the words *Catholic Converts,* you would come up with a list of hundreds of men and women who have become Catholic in recent years. A partial list of the names include Bob Hope, John Wayne, Tony Snow, Sam Brownback, Richard Neuhouse, Robert Novak, Newt Gingrich, Tony Blair, Jeb Bush, Laura Ingraham and even Ali Agca, the Turk who tried to assassinate Saint John Paul II and who, after the *Pope's* ministering to him in prison, converted to the Catholic Faith. Going back a few years, other names of those the Lord has called into the Catholic Faith include John Henry Newman, G. K. Chesterton, Buffalo Bill, Gary Cooper, Dorothy Day, Avery Dulles, Faye Dunaway, Graham Greene, Ronald Knox, Peter Kreeft, Thomas Howard, Malcolm Muggeridge,

Thomas Merton, Bernard Nathanson, Vincent Price, Knute Rockney, J.R.R. Tolkien, and Rabbi Zolli, Chief Rabbi of Rome, who entered the Catholic Faith after World War II because of what Pope Pius XII did to save the Jews.

This is not to overwhelm you with statistics, nor to impress you with "name dropping", nor is it intended to be a "sales pitch" for the Catholic Church! This is basic knowledge of what is happening in the religious sector of our secular culture today. Christian people are loving God, finding him, worshiping him and serving him, but few people ever hear about it! For example, in the news media mention is made of the Catholic Church as the largest Christian religion in the world, the largest charitable organization feeding the poor, clothing the naked, sheltering the homeless with hospitals, nursing homes, schools, and orphanages; but the substantial part played by the Catholic Church in the history and building of this nation since its founding is not considered "newsworthy" by the media, and the Church's activities are practically unnoticed, sometimes ridiculed or worse. I mention this because, though divided by denomination, the Christian Churches are united in their spiritual depths because *Christianity is Christ and he cannot be divided!* So, for example, were you to consider becoming Catholic, being a Bible Christian or perhaps an evangelical, there is nothing you would have to give up! You would not have to give up Bible reading, your personal relationship with the Lord, or your prayer life, and this is because, up to the 1500s, every Christian was Catholic. Were you able to go back through your Protestant genealogy past the 1500s, you would find your ancestors to be Catholic! Steven Ray uses the analogy of children of a family, saying they're going to sleep in the tent set up in the backyard; where do they get the bedding, the equipment and the food? It all comes from their house. Or take the example of a ship in distress whose passengers have to resort to the life rafts; everything taken onto the raft came from the ship. As the reformers of the 1500s followed their new awakenings in religion they took with them what good things they felt they needed from their "House". Everything good that our Protestant brothers and sisters have been received from Christ and the Church, from the "House of God" he founded.

Were you ever to come to the realization that you sensed a calling to the Catholic Faith, in Christian love I would offer these suggestions. The most direct step would be to stop by your local Catholic Church - or one a Catholic friend would suggest - and ask about the RCIA program (The Rite of Christian Initiation for Adults), which is a series of talks on the Catholic religion beginning in September and ending with the feast of Easter. But you could also start with a less direct approach by looking into the *Coming Home Network.* Their website and newsletter would be a big help on your way home to the "faith of your forefathers". *The Coming Home Network* is currently working with 1,700 men and women, mostly ministers, professors, teachers, seminarians from other denominations, that are looking into the Catholic Faith. Among these 1,700, 1,300 are Protestant ministers. Six hundred have already converted to the Catholic Faith in recent years. I have personally listened to a CD with over a hundred conversion stories of former Protestant ministers, many of whom have had to make great sacrifices to become Catholic. Some have had to give up their positions of employment; some have lost friends, or connection with their relatives. I found what is most remarkable and beautiful about these ministers is the fact that not one of them is *anti-Protestant:* they love their former denomination; they love the personal relationship with Jesus that their former denomination has given them; they love the fact that they learned Scripture and have come to know Jesus as their Lord and Savior. And now, as Catholic Christians, being part of the one Church founded by Christ, they claim to be "fulfilled" Christians.

My further suggestion is the remote preparation of spiritual reading. There are many books available that would acquaint you with the Catholic Church, starting with the stories of the recent converts, especially those of the Protestant Ministers. Some titles are *Rome Sweet Home* by Scott and Kimberly Hahn, the three volumes of *Surprised by Truth* by Patrick Madrid, and *Crossing the Tiber* by Steve Ray. There is, of course, the *Catechism of the Catholic Church*, the most informative resource book to have; older classics like *Faith of Our Fathers* by Cardinal Gibbons, *The Faith of Millions* by John O'Brien, *The Spirit of Catholicism* by Karl Adam or the more recent *Fundamentals of the Faith* by Peter Kreeft and *Rediscovering Catholicism* by Matthew Kelly. And if you wouldn't take it too personally, *Catholicism for Dummies* is an excellent book! I leave you with one final note in my Invitation were you to consider "joining my Church": it is not because it is true and deep and beautiful; not because it is philosophical,

theological, intellectual, and so rich in spirituality, art, liturgy, history, and tradition,

which would be yours, of course; not because
it is the original Christian Church, but
because the Catholic Church founded by
Jesus Christ *is* Jesus Christ, living on through
history in the fullness of his Way, Truth and
Life, from the very beginning, here with us
now and "always, until the end of the world."
God bless you on your spiritual journey.

A Mother and Child

A mother and a little child
came into the world and smiled;
earth has never been the same
since they came, with their touch of Spring;
they called him "Little King"
and her "his Undefiled" --
the mother and the little child.

A mother and a growing boy

brought the world a special joy,

sharing all our common ways,

nights and days, as a family:

none knew their destiny --
(earth could have been his toy!) --
the mother and the growing boy.
A mother and a dying son
loved the world with hearts as one;
through his death on Calvary,
humanity is his place to dwell:

earth cries "Emmanuel!

See what their love has done!" --

the mother and the dying son.

Someday when all the worlds are old,

and stories of God's love unfold,

then all who share the vast reward

of Life, of Lord, in that Eternal Spring

will through all Knowing sing

how once a planet smiled

whose past claimed Son and Mother,

whose race became God's Child!

About the Author
Father Francis Joseph Peffley

Father Francis J. Peffley was born March 16, 1963 in Norristown, Pennsylvania to William and Mary Peffley. He graduated from Christendom College in Front Royal, Virginia with a Bachelor of Arts degree in Theology. Father Peffley attended Mount Saint Mary's Seminary in Emmitsburg, Maryland where he received his priestly formation and his Master of Divinity and Master of Arts Degrees. He was ordained to the priesthood for the diocese of Arlington, Virginia on May 19, 1990. Founding pastor of Holy Trinity parish in Gainesville, Virginia, for ten years he served. 3,500 families in a vibrant and rapidly growing community, with 65 ministries and organizations. He is currently serving at St. Mary of Sorrows Parish in Fairfax, Virginia.

In addition to his parish activities Father Peffley is especially active with the parish young adult ministry, marriage preparation, retreat work and pilgrimages,

Catholic apologetics, and evangelization. He serves as Arlington diocesan spiritual director of the Legion of Mary and for the past twenty years has also been chaplain for the Knights of Columbus councils in each of the parishes in which he served. Father Peffley's interests include a "juggling apostolate" (which, among many other items, includes fire torches and machetes!), golf, scuba diving, bowling, billiards, baseball card collecting, and traveling to pilgrimage sites and shrines.

Father Peffley is author of the recently published book, *Inside the Legion of Mary* and has written numerous articles which have appeared in a variety of publications, including the book, *The Priest and the Legion of Mary, Homiletic and Pastoral Review, Queen of All Hearts magazine, Maria Legionis magazine, Lay Witness,* and the *Arlington Catholic Herald.* He has recorded over two hundred CDs on Spirituality, the Saints, Apologetics, Evangelization and the Family. His Sunday and weekday homilies and retreat talks appear online on his website *www.fatherpeffley.org.*

Made in the USA
Middletown, DE
01 December 2019